FAMOUS

Folk from

CO. DOWN

Jane E M Crosbie

BALLYHAY BOOKS

First published by Ballyhay Books,
an imprint of Laurel Cottage Ltd.
Ballyhay, Donaghadee, N. Ireland 2018.
Copyrights Reserved.
© Text Jane E M Crosbie.
All rights reserved.
No part of this book may be reproduced or stored on any media
without the express written permission of the publishers.
Design & origination in N. Ireland.
Printed & bound by Bell & Bain Limited, Scotland
ISBN 978 1 910657 11 9

To Patrat and Lady P.
"You make my Heart Sing"

CONTENTS

INTRODUCTION

Milk Chocolate – that's how this book started.

I've always loved history, ever since I can remember and over the years I have maintained my interest, both professionally and in my leisure time. When everyone on the beach was reading *Fifty Shades of Grey*, I was reading William Hague's excellent biography of William Pitt the Younger because, no matter how well you know a subject, it is always a joy to unearth some fascinating new nugget of information.

Thus when relaxing one day with a cup of coffee, a box of chocolates and an article about County Down man Hans Sloane, I was delighted to find that were it not for Sloane one of my three indulgences might be missing because, the article informed me, Sloane was the man who introduced milk chocolate to the world!

And that got me thinking.... what contributions have other sons and daughters from my home county made to the world?

The answer it turns out is that for a small county in a small country on the edge of Europe, County Down has spawned more than its fair share of men and women who have influenced not only the world in which they lived themselves, but in many cases the world we live in today. And thus the concept of this book arose.

As with any such exercise the first question was who to include and who to leave out and right away I will state that this book does not pretend to be a definitive list of *Famous Folk from County Down*. There were very few rules governing selection (indeed about the only one applied strictly was that being alive at time of writing was grounds for exclusion) and my aim in this book is not to argue the relative merits of one group of high achievers against another, but rather to give a feel for what Co. Down has contributed to the wider world – a balance if you like for our natural tendency to talk ourselves down.

Perhaps at this point a short explanation about the approach I have taken is necessary. I was very fortunate to have had a wonderful history teacher, Alison Jordan, who instilled certain core principles about the approach one should take when looking at the actions of historical personalities.

The most important of these is that one should always guard against judging their actions by modern standards. This is even more important in the current climate of social media storms and the 'woke' generation. Therefore I have included people such as Rollo Gillespie and Sir Hans Sloane, who were involved in or received income from colonial expansion and slavery, without ever once struggling with their conscience. In the seventeenth and eighteenth century slavery was a complicated affair with the exploits of Rollo Gillespie providing fascinating insights. There is no evidence to suggest Gillespie had any moral qualms about slavery although he had first hand experience of most every aspect of it. A senior figure in a colonising power where slavery was a key part of colonial commerce, on several occasions he narrowly evaded capture by slave traders himself and he forged a very good working relationship with Touissant L'Ouverture the leader of the Haitian Slave Revolt, who was both a freed slave and a slave owner. We forget that slavery was not only an accepted form of labour throughout the world but that it was not only confined to the Atlantic slave trade and thousands of Europeans were captured and pressed into slavery by the Barbary slave traders. It should also be remembered that Irish and British MPs in the British House of Commons voted to abolish the Slave Trade in 1812 and the much-maligned Castlereagh was one of the prime movers in the campaign to abolish slavery throughout British overseas territories.

One trait which is shared by many of the people discussed in this book is their lack of respect for authority. Amy Carmichael rejected the attempts of both men and the Church of England to dictate how she could fulfil her mission in India; Harry Ferguson, Frank Pantridge and James Martin spent their adult lives forging their own way in the teeth of bureaucratic and professional disapproval. Even George Best, thought that he knew best.

Nowadays conformity is obliquely encouraged. The inexorable rise of social media, despite it's promises of free speech and empowerment, imposes a rigid herd mentality that vilifies anyone who dares go against the grain and any child who does not fit into the confines of a rigid education system is given a label, whereas the truth is that they might be dreaming up a wonderful new invention and are bored by the lessons. However, many of our greatest men and women achieved what they did by kicking against the traces and going their own way. Our lives would be much reduced if they had been happy to simply conform.

Another trait which emerged was one of personal bravery. Time and again men such as Rollo Gillespie, Robert Ross and of course Blair Mayne, displayed great bravery with no regard for their own personal safety. They were natural leaders on and off the battlefield. But so too were the ancient saints who set off across the North Channel in small curraghs to take their mission to Scotland, England and down as far as Italy. They went unarmed into hostile territory armed only with the conviction that they were doing

God's commandment. It can be argued that this is also the case with two of the women featured in the book, Margaret Byers and Elizabeth Bell. Both took on the political establishment of the day and won. They changed the course of history just as much as Patrick, Pantridge and Castlereagh.

With the exception of the old Irish kings and medieval barons few members of the aristocracy are featured in this book. There is no conscious bias behind this, if there's any point to make, its not where you start but where finish. The fact that Patrick Brontë's parents could barely write their own names and yet his daughters wrote some of the greatest novels in the English language shows how far determination can take someone out of their own path.

Nor have I dwelt upon the political situation pertaining at the time or any unrest, armed revolt etc, unless it directly impacted upon the lives of the individuals under discussion. This book does not pretend to be a political history of the county. However where it is relevant it has been included. For example it was well known that Harry Ferguson assisted in the gunrunning in the early 20th century and it is impossible to discuss Castlereagh without mentioning the politics of the day. For the most part the subject's political opinions were either unknown or did not play an important part in the main achievements of their lives. Likewise their sexuality or religion.

Given that they are missing from most histories other than in walk on parts, I was delighted to be able to include several women amongst my notable personalities. This is not tokenism but rather because by any standards they more than fulfil the brief for this book. Amy Carmichael's legacy is as well known in the missionary world today as it was when she was still alive. Whatever one thinks about the role of missionaries in society the work that she did to rescue children from a life of degradation and sexual exploitation deserves recognition. Similarly Elizabeth Bell deserves recognition, as much for her efforts to achieve the vote for women as for being the first female medical graduate in Ireland. The fact that she was able to gain a medical degree was down to the efforts of another woman, who changed the course of education in Ireland, not just for women, but also for men. Margaret Byers, by insisting that all the teachers at her school, Victoria College, held university degrees or diplomas, raised the standard of women's education far beyond that available elsewhere. It also made the various male schools raise their own standards to meet hers.

And finally, no fulfilled life can be all work and no leisure and so I have included a few figures from the world of entertainment and literature, each of whom continue to enrich our lives today.

I hope that you will enjoy reading this book as much as I enjoyed researching and writing it. Unfortunately it is now over and unless anyone can suggest more notable personalities from the county I will have to go and do the housework that I have managed to avoid over the past few months.

....well perhaps after a cup of coffee and just one chocolate to commemorate Hans Sloane!

SIR HANS SLOANE
1660-1753

Scientist and Collector

Although Sloane trained in and practised medicine he was
obsessed with the natural world, amassing and cataloguing
a huge collection of specimens and materials which were
the basis for British Museum, the British Library and the
Natural History Museum.

He is credited with the invention of milk
chocolate.

As someone who has a bit of a hoarding habit, Sir Hans Sloane
has always been one of my heroes. He took hoarding to a
completely different level, even going as far as buying the next-
door house in Bloomsbury Square just to store his books, prints
and drawings. At the time of his death the collection ran to over
80,000 items, all carefully cross referenced, annotated and catalogued. To give an idea of the scale and range of his collection of
the 1,903 quadrupeds there were the skeletons of 68 Elephants,
20 Rhinos, 8 Hippos and 248 lizards. These jostled for space with
23,000 coins and medals; 4,000 manuscripts and 50,000 books.
And, most importantly of all for some of us, there is a strong case
that he invented milk chocolate!

Hans was born in Fredrick Street, Killyleagh in the year of the
Restoration, 1660, as the youngest of the seven sons born to
Alexander and Sarah Sloane. Alexander was the Receiver General of

taxes for Co. Down and Agent for the Hamilton family and Sarah had arrived in Killyleagh as a companion to Anne Carey, daughter of the Duke of Monmouth, who married James Hamilton, 2nd Viscount Clandeboye and 1st Earl of Clanbrassil. Only two of Sir Hans's brothers survived childhood. One brother, William (1658-1728), was a prosperous merchant who married Jane Hamilton of Killyleagh, who inherited the Earl of Clanbrassil's estate. The other, James (1655-1704) was MP for Killyleagh in the Irish Parliament and then represented Thetford in Norfolk at Westminster (1796-1700) for the Whigs or Crown interests. Ironically, given that his brother's collection was acquired for the nation with the proceeds of a lottery, on 25 April 1799 he voted in favour of a bill to suppress lotteries.

The family were closely connected with the Hamilton family and the young Sloane brothers were educated in the local school which had been set up by the Hamilton family. For most of his childhood, however, the young Hans was free to explore the Strangford shoreline close to his home and even, on one occasion, to visit the Copeland Islands, close to Donaghadee. In a letter written in 1725 to Richard Richardson Sloane recalled his visit to:-

"many small uninhabited islands where the ordinary sea-mews etc have laid their eggs often on the ground, without any or with at least very small nests, so thick, that it was difficult to pass along without treading on them: while the birds made a terrible noise over our heads."

When he was 16 years old Hans's outdoor pursuits were severely curtailed when he developed haemoptysis (coughing blood) and had to remain indoors for the next three years. The massive Hamilton library at Killyleagh Castle was made available to him and it was then that he developed his thirst for knowledge and interest in science. At the age of 19 he was sufficiently recovered to make his way to London to pursue a career in medicine. Armed with a letter of introduction from the Hamiltons he established himself in Water Lane, Blackfriars. In 1683 he moved to France to further his studies in both medicine and botany at the universities in Paris and Montpellier, however he took his actual degree as a Doctor of Physic at the University of Orange (Avignon), because as a protestant Sloane was unable to take his degree at the catholic universities in France.

Throughout his long life Sloane was unusual amongst his contemporaries for his ease with all strata of society. He was equally at home with the greatest minds of the age as he was with lowly sailors and even pirates. Age was not a barrier to friendship either. When he first arrived in London to commence his studies he had made friends with Robert Boyle.

Robert Boyle (1627-1691) was the seventh son of the Earl of Cork and is widely regarded as the father of chemistry [even I have heard of Boyle's Law]. He was a close family friend of the Hamilton family and so may even have known the young Hans before he arrived in London. The connection to Boyle would have opened many doors for the young Irishman and it was through Boyle that he became friends with the celebrated botanist John Ray (1627-1705). These friendships lasted for the men's lifetimes.

On Sloane's return from France he took up residence in lodgings in Fleet Street and in 1625 he was elected to the Royal Society. The President of the Royal Society at the time was the celebrated diarist Samuel Peyps, who became another life long friend and patient. Sloane attended Peyps in his final illness and performed his autopsy. He also became an assistant to the most influential physician of the day, Thomas Sydenham. On 12th April, 1687 Sloane was admitted as a Fellow of the Royal College of Physicians. However Sloane, throughout his medical career, did not only treat the rich and famous. Even when he was attending Queen Anne on her deathbed he was also running a free clinic for poor people, from his own house, every day from 8am to 10am. He often accepted strange objects in lieu of payment from the many sailors who made use of his services.

With such influential friends and acquaintances it was not surprising that the 2nd Duke of Albemarle should have asked Sloane to accompany him to Jamaica as personal physician to his family. What is more surprising is the fact that Sloane accepted the position. Many of his friends pleaded with him not to go for at that time not only was Jamaica on the other side of the world, it might as well have been in another world entirely so fraught was the trip with risk. However John Ray was more enthusiastic and thought that it would be a great opportunity to acquire new specimens of plants. Sloan decided to put his medical career in London on hold and set out for the Caribbean. It was a decision that was to change the course of his life and was to enrich successive generations up to and including our own.

One example of how this trip changed the course of history is that while he was in Jamaica Sloane had collected Sea Beans, a tropical plant native to the area. A few years later, his collection already being famous, he was sent a couple of unknown pods that had been collected from a beach in Orkney to see if he knew what they were, the sender not being sure. Sloane, however, knew exactly what they were – Sea Beans. But how could they have found their way to Orkney, not renowned for its tropical climate?

Sloane came up with a possible explanation which resulted in his writing a scientific paper detailing his theory about the great ocean currents. He argued that rather than just going from left to right and up and down, as was the generally accepted theory of the day, there had to be a powerful current that ran up the Atlantic and curved round the British Isles. If that was accepted to exist, then why not other currents in other large seas and oceans? This theory of the existence of currents was taken up by other scientists and exploited by other explorers, such as Captain Cook, to circumnavigate the world and open up trade routes.

An example of how the influence of his collection stretches through the centuries to the present day is that some scientists are using DNA extracted from his vast seaweed collection to help provide a snapshot of the levels of acid in the oceans in the eighteenth century in an effort to better understand climate trends.

A contemporary account in the Archives of Vaucluse, from the time of his graduation remarks that the young Sloane was *"of medium height, hair very short, light chestnut, face rather long and grave, marked with smallpox."* It is the last remark that perhaps explains his interest in the development of inoculations against Smallpox that were developed later in his career. In the eighteenth century, smallpox accounted for between 10-20% of all deaths in England and so there was a great urgency to find a cure or vaccine but a successful vaccine was only developed by Edward Jenner in 1796.

Prior to that time the main defense against the disease was via variolation. This involved making scratches on the skin of the patient and then rubbing fresh smallpox scabs or pus into the scratches. This caused a moderate to mild outbreak of the disease but thereafter the patient was immune to the disease. Lady Mary Wortley Montague is widely credited with introducing this method of inoculation to England. She had witnessed the method while she was the wife of the British Ambassador to the Ottoman Empire in Constantinople. Sloane recounted that:-

> *"The Princess Anne, now Princess of Orange, fell ill with smallpox in such a dangerous way that I feared for her life. The late Queen Caroline, when Princess of Wales, to secure her other children, and for the common good, begged the lives of six condemned criminals, who had not had smallpox, in order to try the experiment of inoculation on them."*

Throughout his career as a society doctor, scientist and published author Sloane was collecting examples of natural history and everyday life. In 1695 he married the heiress Elizabeth Langley, who had inherited a third of a large sugar plantation in Jamaica. This means that a substantial part of Sloane's income was derived from the exploitation of slave labour and though there is no record of his opinions about slavery, he certainly didn't reject the income it brought him. However, with his obsessive collecting mania, he collected and carefully catalogued numerous items associated with slavery and in later generations these and his accounts of the conditions on the sugar plantations pertaining during his visit there in the late 1680s, were used by William Wilberforce to argue for the abolition of slavery and the slave trade.

Given his large income, he was able to increase his collection by outbidding others as various collections came up for sale. So he acquired the Charlton Collection in 1702, the Plunket Collection in 1710, the Hermann Collection in 1711, the Kaempfer Collection in 1717 and the Petiver Collection in 1718. His long-suffering wife and daughters moved out of Bloomsbury Place altogether and set up house in Chelsea.

Hidden in the Natural History Museum's collection is one of the oldest specimens of a cocoa bean in the world. This was picked by Hans Sloane himself during his visit to Jamaica in 1687. It was from this bean, or rather its long-gone companions, that Sir Hans Sloane gave the nation what I would argue (as an unreformed addict) was his greatest gift. Milk Chocolate.

Of course Hans Sloane did not 'invent' chocolate. The native people of the Americas have that accolade. Nor was he the person who introduced chocolate to Europeans. That goes to the Spanish. But it was Sir Hans who added milk to the mixture and marketed it as a healthy alternative to alcohol. Its reputation grew and was soon being sold in coffee houses and cafes throughout London as one of the earliest examples of a branded product. His recipe for milk chocolate was subsequently bought by two brothers, called Cadbury and the rest, as they say, is history.

If Hans Sloane were alive today he would probably have been diagnosed with a obsessive, compulsive disorder and hyperactivity. His vast collection was carefully catalogued, annotated and cross-referenced in his own hand. The collection's fame grew throughout his life and even during his own lifetime people would flock to see his 'curiosities'. There is a story about him receiving a visit from the composer George Frideric Handel, 1685-1759, to see the collection. Sloane was enraged when Handel placed a hot buttered crumpet on a manuscript, although Handel maintained that it was because of the waste of butter.

Sloane was determined that the collection should remain intact and available to the public after his death and so he stated that it should be offered to the nation for the sum of £20,000. If after six months the money had not been found then it was to be offered in turn to St. Petersburg, Paris, Madrid and finally Berlin. Parliament decided to run a National Lottery, which was very successful and raised £300,000 (£25,500,00 today) and the collection was saved for the nation. To display it correctly it was split in three and thus was born the British Museum, the British Library and the Natural History Museum, all of which remain free to visit, just as Sloane intended.

He collected, amongst other things, Plants; seeds; coins; medals; prints; drawings; shoes; animal skins; musical instruments; books; manuscripts; statues; fossils; and ethnographic objects. So vast is it that even today it is still relatively unexplored.

Dr Mark Spencer, curator of Botany at the Natural History Museum chose Sir Hans Sloane as his Natural History Hero on the BBC Radio 4 programme of the same name. He said of Sir Hans that *"The gifts he gave to the nation in the 18th century helped form the way museums developed over the next 250 years. Just for that he is an extraordinary man."*

Not a bad legacy for a little boy from Killyleagh. Oh, and he invented Milk Chocolate.

MAJOR-GENERAL SIR ROLLO GILLESPIE

1766-1814

Soldier and adventure

In an astonishing career he would see action from the Carribean to India, stopping of along the way for numerous duels and other brushes with death. His statue which overlooks Comber remains the only Masonic public monument in Ireland.

Sir Rollo Gillespie's life story reads like the script for every Regency film starring Stewart Granger or adventure novel ever written. He managed to pack more adventure into 48 years of life than even the most intrepid of modern heroes. He fought duels, escaped capture by donning women's clothing, evaded being sold into slavery and much, much more. Imagine a cross between Captain Jack Sparrow and the Scarlet Pimpernel and you are almost half way there.

Rollo was born into an Anglo-Irish gentry family in Comber in 1766. His father had been married three times and Rollo was his only surviving child. Subsequently, as his biographer Major Sir William Thorn is at pains to point out, the young Rollo *experienced from the fondest of parents every indulgence*. He was sent to school at Norland House in Kensington with the intention that he would eventually attend university and take up a career at the Bar. This aspiration was halted in its tracks after the family took a house in Bath for the school holidays. Major Thorn is convinced that this holiday

'instead of training the mind to constant discipline and patient investigation ... (gave) an excessive latitude to the passions and ... opened perpetually new scenes of pleasures to the imagination.'

He places the blame firmly at the door of his fond parents

'Accustomed to the unlimited gratification of his wishes from his very childhood, and thus habituated at the most critical period of life to scenes of extravagance in this receptacle of the wealthy and idle, the weak and designing, it is not at all to be wondered that he should return to school with a lessened inclination to study.'

So it should not surprise us that on 28th April 1783 the young Rollo, not yet 18, was bought a commission in the 3rd Regiment Irish Horse Carbineers.

And so began a life of adventure that would be scarcely creditable if it were not backed up by official documents.

While stationed in Ireland he met his future wife, Miss Annabelle Taylor, while out riding near Clogher. Within a couple of months the 'eager couple proceeded on the wings of love' to Dublin where they were married by private license. Neither couple had the consent of their parents and so had to keep the marriage secret until Rollo could convince his parents of its merits. The doting parents agreed at once and welcomed Annabelle into their family. Shortly afterwards, in 1786, Rollo fought his first recorded duel. Two men that he knew had challenged each other to a duel and Rollo was present as the second to one of them. The men exchanged shots and neither man was injured. That should have been the end of the matter but then the other man (his name has been lost to the mists of time) became involved in a violent argument with Rollo and challenged him to a duel. Rollo accepted and shot and killed him. At this time duelling, although discouraged was still legal and there were various legal niceties one of which was that the dying man should forgive the other. This he refused to do, so technically Rollo was guilty of murder. He and his own second escaped via Donaghadee to the country houses of various friends in Scotland and England, before they both returned to Dublin to stand trail, in 1788. So impressed were the judge and jury that they had voluntarily returned for trail that they immediately found them not guilty of murder and returned a verdict of justifiable homicide.

Before recounting a few highlights from Rollo's military career it is important to set them in their historical context. Britain had recently lost the American colonies and consequently was not sure whether she actually wanted an Empire per se. However successive governments were very sure that they did not want France to have one. In fact British foreign policy at this time can be summed up in a sentence – Establish free trade through spheres of influence and, at all costs, stop the French. This is why Rollo, in 1794 found himself swimming, sword clamped firmly between his teeth, towards the French held fort in Port-au-Prince, in the Carribbean.

In 1792, leaving Annabelle with his doting mother, Rollo was transferred to the 20th Light Dragoon Guards with the rank of Lieutenant to serve on the island of Jamaica and rapidly gained promotion to the rank of Captain. In 1794, having survived both a ship wreck and yellow fever, Rollo was sent to help wrestle control of Saint-Domingue [Haiti] from revolutionary French control. While laying siege to Port-au-Prince it was:-

> 'thought proper to send a flag of truce to the commissioner, Santhonax, demanding a surrender of the place. The mission ... was readily undertaken by Captain Gillespie and Captain Rowley (RN) both of whom were fired at in attempting to swim to the shore, with their swords in their mouths.'

Both men were taken prisoner by Santhonax, who immediately decided that they were spies and so ordered that they should be shot. As he faced a firing squad, Gillespie noticed that Santhonax was wearing a Masonic symbol and, being himself a Mason, made *'one of the signs peculiar to the order, and that in a way which could not be overlooked by the irritated republican.'* The ruse worked and, while he refused their offer of surrender, Santhonax halted the execution and instead gave them both a meal and a bed for the night before releasing them, unharmed, the next day. Santhonax would have been better advised to have accepted the offer of surrender as the city fell to the British forces after a hard fought battle. Rollo was described as having fought bravely during this battle but was sufficiently injured as to merit a trip home to visit his family. Again he suffered a ship wreck, this time in the English Channel and then at the end of his leave en-route to rejoin his regiment when he got into an altercation in Cork, assaulting a man he had met at the theatre who refused to stand for the National Anthem. The man pressed charges which necessitated Gillespie seeking refuge in the houses of friends and donning the disguise of women's clothing before he returned to the ship taking him back to Jamaica.

Britain eventually decided to withdraw from Saint-Domingue and Rollo helped to negotiate the peaceful evacuation of all civilians by working closely with the legendary Toussaint Louverture.

The best-known leader of the Haitian Revolution, Toussaint L'Ouverture was a freed slave who, as a plantation owner with slaves of his own, was a fascinating figure who illustrates the fluidity of colonial life at this time. He took a leading role in the Slave Revolt of 1791 and eventually secured the freedom of what became Haiti from Napoleonic France. Major Thorn presumably quotes Rollo when he says of Toussaint that he had *"the peculiar merit of deserving the confidence reposed in him, as much by the excellence of his private character as by his personal bravery and military judgement"*.

It was while he was still in Saint-Domingue that Rollo was involved in one of the most famous of all his many adventures. He was sleeping upstairs in his own house when he was woken up by the screams of his personal servant. Grabbing his sword he ran down stairs to discover that the house was being attacked by eight heavily armed men. His servant's arm was almost severed at the shoulder. Not only did Rollo take on all eight them, he killed six and severely wounded the other two. Rollo himself was severely injured but Major Thorn assures us that *'Medical aid being speedily procured, this brilliant ornament of his profession was snatched from the jaws of the grave.'*

Rollo spent a number of years in Jamaica where he rose to be in charge of the garrison. On his return to England he was once again in trouble – this time in a court-marshal as a result of a malicious allegation of fraud.

In 1800 a Major Allen Cameron had arrived at the garrison in Jamaica. Rollo, by this time a Colonel, had instituted certain reforms to the garrison and had increased the medical bill allowance and also the amount available for food. Major Cameron took copies of the books and once the regiment returned back to England started court marshal proceedings against Rollo. However Major Cameron had failed to take into account the fact that the regiment, while in Jamaica, was paid for by the Jamaican authorities, not the Crown, and they had been more than happy to pay the extra expenses as the regiment's health, and therefore ability to function, had improved dramatically. In fact so dramatic had been this improvement that when the regiment had arrived back in England it had paraded in front of the Duke of York who was amazed at how well they looked as regiments returning from the Caribbean were usually physical wrecks. Rollo was able to take comfort from the fact that the court was inundated with testimonials from all his superior officers as well as the Jamaican authorities extolling his virtues, not only as an officer but also as a person and he was unanimously cleared.

Deciding that a change was as good as a rest Gillespie made a transfer to the 19th Light Dragoons, a cavalry regiment that were formed specifically to serve in India in defense of 'British' trading posts and forts. Created in 1781, they were not part of the East India Company's private army but were part of the British Army. Perhaps the most famous solider connected with the regiment was Arthur Wellesely, later Duke of Wellington.

Understandably, given that he had survived two ship wrecks, Gillespie decided to make his way overland to meet up with his new regiment. This was by no means the safest option and on his way there he was saved from assassination in Germany by the exiled United Irishman Napper Tandy, escaped being sold into slavery by an Ottoman ferryman, fought another duel in Constantinople, saved the life of an Arab Sheik in Aleppo, and was given an Arab stallion by Ali Pasha in Baghdad. He finally arrived in India in early 1806.

At this time India was not a colony. Instead it was a sphere of interest. Now it can be argued 'tomato tomato' but the East India Company [the EIC] was technically in charge having made trading agreements with the various Indian rulers, which were later backed up by what was in effect the largest private standing army in the world. This army was largely Indian, although the senior officers were usually European. The British government gradually took more and more control of the EIC until, in the mid nineteenth century, they eventually took over all control in India. There was a lot of criticism of the EIC, not least from Robert Clive who said,

> *"We still talk about the British conquering India, but that phrase disguises a more sinister reality. It was not the British government that seized India at the end of the 18th century, but a dangerously unregulated private company headquartered in one small office, five*

windows wide, in London, and managed in India by an unstable sociopath"

No sooner had Gillespie arrived at his garrison at Arcot than he was involved in more drama. Colonel Fancourt, an old friend from Jamaica, was stationed nearby in Vellore fort and asked him over to dine. He was unable to go to dinner but decided to go for breakfast. As he made his way there a message reached him that the Sepoy troops at the fort had mutinied and were massacring all the British inhabitants. Telling the messenger to get help from the 19th at Arcot, Rollo rode on ahead to try to rescue his friend. When he arrived at the fort the few remaining British troops were confined to part of the ramparts. He recognized one of them as a Sergeant Brodie, who had served with him in Jamaica, and asked him to link together belts so that he could climb up to join in the battle. This he did and led a bayonet charge, which drove the mutineers back sufficiently to allow the defenders to blow open the gates, thus allowing the 19th Light Dragoons to ride in to the rescue. Unfortunately Colonel Fancourt had been hacked to pieces, which may explain, but does not excuse, Rollo's decision to execute approximately 100 defeated mutineers. In total the mutineers had killed over 200 men, women and children in the Vellore fort but Thorn argues that this was supposed to be the start of a wider mutiny and by thwarting it Rollo had actually managed to stop the mutiny before it really got started.

The years 1811 to 1814 saw Rollo in command of the invasion of Java, which defeated a combined force of approximately 17,000 French, Dutch and local troops, and killing a French Colonel in hand-to-hand combat. He was not overly impressed by the famous Stamford Raffles, who had been appointed Lieutenant Governor of Java and asked to be transferred back to India.

Shortly after his return to India, and newly promoted to Major General, he was instructed to assist the East India Company in their attempt to bring the kingdom of Nepal within their 'sphere of influence'. He organised a four prong attack involving 4,500 British and Indian troops, on the Nepalese hill fort at Khalanga, defended by around 600 Gurkhas. This was not as one sided as it might appear as the fort was in a very good strategic position and the Gurkhas were and remain a revered and feared fighting force. On 31st October 1814, as he was urging his section of the troops to attack he turned to Charles Pratt Kennedy, a fellow Ulsterman, and cried *"Now Charles! One shot more for the honour of Down".* As Major Thorn describes *"Within a few paces of the wall, he was shot through the heart and instantly expired."* Such was his influence that the British forces, on learning of his death, immediately retreated. He was posthumously knighted with a KCB on 1 January 1815.

On 24 June 1845 with over 50 Masonic lodges present, the Irish Masonic Order unveiled a monument to him on the site of his childhood home, in the town square in Comber. It was and remains the only Masonic public monument in Ireland.

Rollo inspired great loyalty among his friends and respect from his enemies. He was devoted to the men under his command and they to him. I will leave the last word to his biographer and friend Major Thorn.

> *Rollo Gillespie was 'a character who, when all reasonable allowance is made for ordinary imperfections, may be termed a luminary of the first order in the military sphere and a brilliant ornament of human nature.'*

HARRY FERGUSON
1884-1960

Engineer

Born on a farm near Dromore, Ferguson was to become a
towering figure in the mechanisation of agriculture. His
inventions facilitated the huge expansion in agricultural
output required to feed burgeoning populations
throughout the world.

Harry Ferguson was the fourth of eleven children, eight boys
and three girls, born to James and Mary Ferguson. His parents were Plymouth Brethren and while his father was *'an austere bearded, wrath-of-God figure who exercised the sternest discipline on his family'*, his mother was softer and came from an enlightened Newry family. Her half sister Elizabeth Gould Bell was the first woman to graduate in Medicine in Ireland and was a leading suffragette. Her other half-sister and her brother were also doctors. The Fergusons owned a large 100 acre farm at Growell, Dromore and the entire family was expected to help, something that grated on Harry, but did give him an appreciation for the difficulties of horse driven ploughing and reaping.

All books other than the Bible were banned in the household and the young Ferguson and his sisters used to smuggle other reading material in to read under the bedclothes at night. Ferguson received a basic education at two local schools and was not expected or encouraged to stay on after the age of 14. Instead he was expected to start working full time on the farm. He had absolutely no interest in either farming or religion, all of which exasperated relations with his unyielding father. His frustration took the form of cantankerous behaviour and he frequently started violent arguments with visiting lay preachers, who were staying with the family. No doubt everyone gave a large sigh of relief when his older brother Joe, who owned a car and cycle repair garage on the Shankill Road in Belfast, offered him an apprenticeship and it was accepted.

Once he had settled in Belfast, Ferguson discovered that he had a talent for tuning engines. One of his first successes was with a gas engine in the garage that was used to turn lathes and other equipment. It was always overheating and filling the small space with steam, so Harry stayed on late one evening identifying and fixing the problem. This first success stayed with him and 50 years later he mentioned it in a letter to his brother Joe. *'I still remember how 'gunked' you looked.'* Not everything was plain sailing and Ferguson often told the story of how the first time he got behind the wheel of a car he managed to skid it (and the owner who was sitting in the passenger seat) through a shop window.

In an effort to learn more about the technical side of his chosen trade he attended night classes at the Belfast Technical College where he met his life-long friend and business partner John Lloyd Williams. It was also in these early years in Belfast that he became friends with T. McGregor Greer, a wealthy landowner with a passion for cars. This friendship was of vital importance to him when seeking to establish his own independent business as Greer helped him financially.

Ferguson had a fascination with speed and the early years of the twentieth century were an age of discovery in motor vehicles of all types. As early as 1904 he started doing time trials with motorbikes, competing on his own bike but always making sure to include the name of the business in any newspaper reports. Time trials were held in Bangor with bikes tackling the surprisingly steep ascent and descent of Central Avenue. In 1908 he and John Williams travelled to air shows at Rheims and Blackpool. While there he took measurements of the planes on display and returned to Belfast determined to build and fly his own plane. He persuaded his long-suffering brother Joe that it would be a great advertisement for the family business.

Late in 1909 the people of Belfast were no doubt intrigued to see the curious sight of the fuselage of a plane being towed along the Lisburn Road. The wings and tail had been detached and placed in the back of the car. Ferguson was taking his prototype out to Hillsborough Park, the home of Lord Downshire. The next few days were beset with frustration as both equipment and weather conspired against him. However on the 31st December 1909 the late edition of the Belfast Telegraph reported that:

> *The aeroplane rose into the air at a height from nine to twelve feet, amidst the hearty cheers of the onlookers. The poise of the machine was perfect and Mr Ferguson made a splendid flight of 130 yards ... Then he brought the machine to earth safely after having accomplished probably the most successful initial flight that has ever been attempted upon an aeroplane.'*

Harry Ferguson had written himself into the history books as the first person in the Ireland to build and fly his own aeroplane. He informed the Flight magazine that he intended to be the first person to fly the Irish channel, which resulted in a heated discussion in the letters page, with Ferguson proving more than able to defend himself.

The first flight was quickly followed by a flight of over a mile at Massarene Park, Co. Antrim in April 1910 and another of over two and a half miles at a height of 40 feet at Magilligan Strand in June 1910.

However it was the Grand Aerial Display and Sports Meeting at Newcastle on 23rd July 1910 that really made his name. Co-incidentally it was also one of the occasions when the paths of James Martin and Harry Ferguson crossed. The organisers of the Display had offered a prize of £100 (the modern day equivalent of roughly £11,000) to the first person to fly the distance of 3 miles. Ferguson was the only entrant. Yet again he was beset with both mechanical and meteorological difficulties. The adverse weather conditions were such that the deadline for the attempt was extended by a month. He made repeated attempts, going through 3 propellers, 3 wheels and 2 wings in the process. His lack of success resulted in the early twentieth century version of trolling as he received postcards mocking his failure with almost every post. One was addressed to *'H. Ferguson Esq, Aviator on the Ground'* and another to *'Lord Swank Ferguson, Bluff Aviator.'*

Eventually on the 8th August he successfully flew from Dundrum Bay to Newcastle and back again.

In October 1910 he had a very bad crash when the *'plane was hit by turbulence and he was knocked unconscious'.* Colin Fraser in his excellent biography *Harry Ferguson; Inventor and Pioneer* puts the crash down to pilot incompetence rather than a design flaw and certainly the plane was repaired and flown for another 3 years before being destroyed in a crash in 1913 when it was piloted by John Williams. The only parts of it that survived were the engine and the seat.

By the time of the final demise of his first plane Ferguson had parted company with his brother Joe. He had too dominant a personality to be happy playing second fiddle to anyone, let alone his brother. With the backing of McGregor Greer, he opened his own garage May Street Motors in 1913. Such was the bad feeling between the brothers that he was not allowed to use the family name, however as his own fame grew he later changed the garage's name to Harry Ferguson Ltd.

The way in which he ran his first business demonstrates the sort of man he was and why he had so many problems co-operating with business partners, from Henry Ford onwards, over the years. As one former employee said 'Ferguson was a terribly fussy and pernickety man. Cleanliness was a way of life to him.' He insisted that everything in the garage had to be clean. Employees were expected to be very punctual and to wear clean overalls. If their overalls became dirty during a job, they had to be changed. Cars had to be lined up precisely on a chalk mark. All tools had to be kept neat, clean and tidy. He argued that if a tool was always replaced in the same place at the end of each job then time could be saved.

It was as much to do with this attention to detail as his own fame that meant that the business became a great success, indeed so successful that he was able to turn his mind towards the idea of matrimony. In 1913 he married Maureen Watson, who he had known from childhood. She was also a Plymouth Brethren but her parents were less than enthusiastic about the match. Ferguson's teenage outbursts against the visiting lay-preachers had not been forgotten. In the end, and in the teeth of great parental opposition, they were married in the Town Hall in Newry, with his maternal Bell relations in attendance.

Fraser says that Ferguson would not allow Maureen to wear a wedding ring as he saw it as a symbol of ownership or slavery. Perhaps he had been influenced by the views of his maternal aunt Dr Elizabeth Bell, who was a leading suffragette. Maureen, while she usually supported him, even when he was wrong, quietly bought herself a ring. Given that Ferguson's personality was such that he usually fell out with most people he met, he and Maureen enjoyed a very happy and long marriage. While she gave him her undivided support in everything he did, he always said that the only reason why he gave up flying was because she did not like it. Ferguson paid tribute to Maureen in his last Will and Testament when he wrote

'Any success I have had in business during my life I attribute in fair proportion to the loving and solicitous co-operation of my wife and to her loyal companionship, partnership and unvarying devotion in all this that concerned us.'

Ferguson was an unapologetic Ulster Unionist. During the Home Rule crisis immediately preceding the First World War he took an active part in the UVF gunrunning. When the Mountjoy II sailed into Larne harbour under cover of darkness and after a cat and mouse chase with the Royal Navy, he was one of the men who helped to transport her illegal cargo to safe houses throughout the Province. He was a great admirer of Lord Carson and Fraser recounts a story of how, in later life and on a visit home from England, he stood in the driving rain admiring the new statue of his hero in the grounds of Stormont. However, when Churchill offered him a knighthood for his services to agriculture he turned it down, saying that he did not approve of rewarding industrialists with national honours.

Unlike James Martin, Ferguson was not the sort of inventor who tinkered at a workbench. As Colin Fraser notes *'throughout his life he though in terms of overall principles, of concepts, and he therefore needed a designer.'* He did not have any farther to look than his own garage for Willie Sands, a gifted natural engineer and designer. Fraser admits that *'without in any way belittling the genius of Harry Ferguson, it must be plainly stated that Willie Sand's contribution to his achievements was fundamental.'*

Without the food shortages experienced in the final years of the First World War as German attacks on trans Atlantic shipping increased, Ferguson and Sands may well now be remembered as innovative car designers. However it was at this time that the man who couldn't flee his own family farm fast enough first turned his attention to the design of a better tractor and plough.

As more and more men and horses were stripped from the land to feed the war effort in France, even the most conservative of farmers recognised that something would have to change.

There had been tractors before this time, but they were huge, heavy and very expensive designed with a view to pulling implements in place of a team of horses. Ferguson soon realised that the heart of any solution would involve regarding the tractor and the plough as a single unit and so set about designing a plough made specifically to be fitted to the Eros tractor which was essentially a modified Model-T Ford.

This led to Ferguson's first dealings with the Ford company long predating the famous 'handshake' agreement. Almost as soon as Ferguson had put the plough into production Ford started manufacturing a new Fordson tractor at Cork where Henry Ford's father had been born. When Ferguson heard that Charles Sorenson, Ford's right-hand man, was visiting London, he and Sands travelled over with the plans for their plough. With typical directness he greeted Sorenson with the forthright statement *'Your Fordson's all right as far as it goes, but it doesn't really solve any of the fundamental problems.'* It was shortly after this meeting that, despite some opposition from his investors in Belfast, Ferguson and Sands designed and started production on a new improved plough with a patented Duplex hitch to fit the new Fordson tractor. The new design overcame some of the inherent, potentially fatal, problems which arose when farming with the traditional ploughs and tractors of the time and Ferguson decided to travel to America to show it to Henry Ford.

The Ford plant at Dearborn on the Rouge River was a million miles away from Ferguson's own set-up in Belfast. Iron ore was unloaded from the dock at one end of the plant and finished vehicles rolled out at the other end. The first meeting between the two men was not an unqualified success. While Ford was very impressed with the plough and hitch, he thought that Ferguson was either trying to sell him the patents or auditioning for a job. He was amazed when Ferguson refused increasingly high offers for both his invention and his talent. The two men parted without an agreement but with a great respect for each other's character and integrity. As Fraser says *'Both men had met their equals in stubbornness'*. They agreed to stay in touch.

After several false starts he eventually found a production partner in the company owned by the Sherman brothers of Evansville, NY and the company of Ferguson-Sherman Inc was set up in December 1925. The company was successful for a few years but the decision of the Ford Company to stop production of the Fordson tractor sounded the death-knell in 1928. They were able to sell their stock but the company was dissolved. For the next few years Ferguson attempted to find a new partner closer to home. He and his design team of Sands and McGregor Greer worked on various new designs of ploughs and implements that could be attached to existing tractor designs. However there were two main problems: there was a worldwide economic depression and the existing tractors were too heavy. While there wasn't much that he could do about the first of these problems there was something he could do about the second. Design his own tractor.

Progress initially was slow as various blind alleys were explored and discounted. However with Ferguson's fertile mind (he often came up with his best ideas when pacing the floor at night) and the practical engineering skills of Sands, a solution which they called the Ferguson system seemed to solve the problems although as Ferguson admitted himself *'The System was like the Scot who, on receiving his change after paying for his tot in a pub, said, 'It's richt, mind ye, but only jist.'*

Efforts to have the improved plough he'd invented previously man-ufactured on a large scale had seen Ferguson in dispute with various business partners. Despite this he set up a new sales company called Harry Ferguson Ltd and entered into a partnership with David Brown who would produce what was called the Brown-Ferguson tractor in their Huddersfield plant. The Ferguson's rented a house close by and caused a bit of a stir locally by hiring a butler – no doubt eyebrows were raised in Belfast at this extravagance.

The first tractor, by now painted battleship grey, was available in 1936 and one of the first customers was David Lloyd George, the former Prime Minister. Ferguson did not just sell tractors but a complete package. Customers were offered a two-week course on how to use and maintain their tractor – the first of its kind in the UK – and Ferguson's eye for detail and obsession with minimalist efficiency was to be seen everywhere. The tractor was built using only two sizes of bolts and came with a double ended spanner to fit. The spanner was also exactly the same length as the width of a normal furrow slice – and was marked off in inches so that the driver could use it as a measure when making field adjustments.

Ever the sales man, Ferguson made a tour of agricultural shows demonstrating the versatility of the new tractor and, once con-vinced that it would save them time and money, farmers were ea-gerly placing orders.

Despite his success, Ferguson was convinced that only large vol-ume production at low prices would enable his inventions to be marketed on such a scale as to make an impact on agriculture, and in particular on the lives of farmers. With this in mind he continuously exhorted Brown to reduce his price on the tractor and increase production. Brown refused and started designing a heavier tractor, but thought that he was keeping this a secret from Ferguson. When his own men informed him about the new trac-tor, Ferguson appeared quite calm. And well he might. He had remained in contact with the Sherman brothers in the USA and it was Eber Sherman who brought Ferguson's new tractor to Ford's attention.

Like Ferguson, Ford was a farmer's son and was equally committed to making the farmer's life easier and more profitable. He had been trying to repeat the success of the Fordson when he was put back in touch with Ferguson. For his part Ferguson didn't bother to inform David Brown of his plans when, in October 1938, he took a new tractor and all the attachments over to Belfast, from whence he shipped them to Dearborn, Detroit. At three o'clock one afternoon soon after his arrival he, Ford and a couple of others were all gathered in Mrs Ford's fruit garden for the demonstration. Legend has it that after only 5 minutes Ford called a halt to the demonstration and said that he would buy it. However, the reality was that he had arranged for a comparison between several other tractors, which the little grey Ferguson easily outperformed.

When, not having learnt his lesson of over a decade earlier, Ford offered a huge sum in return for the patents Ferguson was blunt. 'You haven't got enough money, because they are not for sale at any price, to you or anybody else,'

'Well, I'm determined to go into the business, and you need me and I need you. So what do you suggest?' asked Ford. 'A gentlemen's agreement.' And so as the two farmer's sons sat in the late autumn sunshine they thrashed out an agreement and, standing up, shook hands on it. Despite the best efforts of all the corporate men it was an agreement that worked to the financial benefit of both parties until Ford died in 1947. After his death the corporate men took over and the whole thing collapsed in acrimony and legal suits.

Both Ford and Ferguson were ideas men. They were also shrewd businessmen who had developed a gut instinct for whom they could trust. Ford trusted Ferguson to be straight with him, so he was straight with Ferguson and vice versa. The same could not be said for Ferguson's dealings with David Brown. As we have seen Brown was developing a new tractor without consulting his partner. For his part Ferguson returned from America but failed to mention his new deal with Ford. When Brown unveiled his new tractor, Ferguson chose to see this as a breach of their contract and demanded that Brown buy him and his fellow Northern Irish investors out of the company, which Brown did. It was after this had all been signed, sealed and delivered that Ferguson revealed his new partnership. He had been such a difficult, cantankerous and infuriating business partner that Brown was just relieved to see him go.

To build and fly your own plane, even today takes a great degree of personal courage and determination, let alone in 1909, when it was made out of wood and Ulster linen. To get back into that plane, after being knocked unconscious and suffering numerous broken bones also took a great deal of courage. However with great age, so for many comes a more cautious approach to life, and a greater appreciation of our own mortality. No doubt as the disgruntled former employee of the Sunset Lodge in Jamaica watched the 73 year old Harry and Mrs Ferguson eating their early evening meal at 7pm before retiring to bed at 9, he thought that they would be easily scared at the sight of a pistol and offer no resistance. And so, disguising himself with a long robe, he woke Ferguson up by hitting him over the head and demanding that he open up the safe in the hotel room. Rather than meekly acquiescing, and despite being shot just below the knee and forty years older than his assailant, Ferguson 'leapt for the door and yanked it open, shouting in his most imperious voice, 'Get the hell out of this. You won't get any money from me.' Meanwhile Maureen was calmly phoning down to reception to tell them that there appeared to be an armed man in their room and could they please send someone up to sort it out. The would-be thief was caught and at his trial alleged that he had been 'savagely attacked' by Ferguson. As Fraser notes 'a number of Ferguson's acquaintances thought humorously that it might have been true.'

In 1947 Harry and Maureen had bought Abbotswood, a stately home in Gloucestershire and it was here that the Ulsterman was to spend the rest of his life. Although much of his time was spent at the factory he would often visit the Silverstone motor circuit to watch the races and chat with the mechanics and drivers. On one occasion he 'was still on the starting grid talking to a driver after the signal to clear the track of non-participants had sounded. … Only the announcer saying, 'If Mr Ferguson would be good enough to leave the track we'll start the race,' finally moved him.'

Perhaps as a result of his growing commercial success and the numerous legal disputes into which he entered with erstwhile business partners (too complicated to go into in this essay) Ferguson was prone to both clinical depression and insomnia. He was prescribed sleeping tablets and on occasion his depression was such that it was treated with electric shock treatment. While that seems barbaric to the modern eye it was considered advanced treatment at the time and he claimed that it did help, although his appearance and listless demeanor shocked his daughter Betty after one of these sessions.

On the morning of 25th October 1960 Harry Ferguson was discovered lying under the water of his bath by his devoted wife. He had died from an overdose of barbiturate tablets and as there was no evidence that he had intended to take his own life, an open verdict was returned at the inquest. As he had requested, Maureen had his body cremated and the ashes scattered over Abbotswood from an aeroplane.

Harry Ferguson was a complex man. He had a talent for antagonizing people, as he was immensely confident in his own talents. As far as he was concerned there were two ways of doing anything he turned his hand to - his way or the wrong way. He fell out with most people that he worked with, including family members and yet enjoyed a long, devoted and happy marriage. Even in his old age he was able to display great personal courage, but was unable to face down his own demons.

Had it not been for the outbreak of the First World War, and the need to increase agricultural production, Harry Ferguson might have gone down as a footnote in the history of the early years of mechanical engineering in Ireland. All that changed in 1917 when he reviewed how a tractor and a plough should work together. From then on the man who had run away from the farm, was to have his name connected to agriculture throughout the world. There is not a country in the world where the Ferguson tractor is unknown. It revolutionized farming, not only in Ferguson's own beloved Co. Down, but throughout the world enabling a burgeoning population to be fed.

DR ELIZABETH
GOULD BELL
1862 - 1934

Medicine and Emancipation

She was the first female medical graduate in Ireland and was one of the first female doctors to be enrolled by the army.

A committed suffragette, she spent time in prison in London after throwing stones through the windows of a major department store.

I have a confession to make, prior to beginning to research this book the only thing that I knew about Dr Elizabeth Gould was that, along with Henrietta Rosetta Neill, she was one of the two first women to graduate in medicine in Ireland. However, as my research continued into people as diverse as Harry Ferguson and Margaret Byers I kept seeing her name, which made me curious, and so I decided to do a quick internet search to find out more about her and was delighted with the results. While her name is not as well known as the others in this book it should be and if only for that reason I have decided to include her story.

Elizabeth Gould Bell was born at Spring Hill House, Newry. Her father Joseph Bell was the Clerk of the Newry Poor Law Union and Elizabeth and her two sisters and two brothers were brought up close to the Workhouse. Her father's other claim to fame is that he was the grandfather of Harry Ferguson. Elizabeth and Harry's mother Mary were half sisters. They couldn't have had a more different adult life. Mary's husband was a dour, Plymouth Brethren who banned books from his household. Elizabeth was a Suffragette, an army doctor and a General Practitioner in Belfast.

While I have not been able to discover where she received her early education, it was thanks to the efforts of Isabella Tod, Margaret Byers and the rest of the Belfast Ladies' Institute that Elizabeth and her sister Margaret and three other young women were able to enrol at the Medical Faculty at Queen's College, Belfast in 1889. Dr Bell graduated MB BCh BAO from the Queen's College, Royal University of Ireland on 27 October 1893. Her name was included in the Medical Directory of Ireland on 25th November, 1893.

The first few years of her life after graduation followed what could be said to have been a predictable course. On 2nd March 1896 she married Hugh Fisher who had been a fellow medical student at Queen's College and they set up home and a general medical practice in Great Victoria Street, Belfast. Their son, Hugo, was born on the 5th April 1898. It was a personal tragedy that was to send her life down less conventional lanes. On 18th October 1901, just five years after their wedding, Hugh died of typhoid fever, no doubt caught in the course of his work. Elizabeth was left as a single parent and so had to work full time.

It is not surprising given her childhood exposure to the harsher aspects of poverty and the Newry Workhouse that Elizabeth should, in addition to her general practice, be involved in various institutions that sought to provide medical care for the women that most people shunned. The unmarried mothers, the drunks, the prostitutes. She provided medical care at the Malone Midnight Mission, which provided homeless women with a bed for a night and later developed into a maternity hospital. Committee members and volunteers would go out at midnight each evening, as the bars were emptying offering assistance where it was necessary. They also provided maternity care for those who could not afford to pay for it or had nowhere else to go. Not all the women who availed of its services were unmarried or drunk. Many poor married women, who in the days before the NHS had nowhere else to go other than the Workhouse, were given maternity care and left with their babies. For those that were not in a position to keep their babies, the Mission arranged for foster care and adoption. The Minute book for the Mission entry for 13th May 1942 recorded that *'One man who adopted one of the babies had himself been born in the home 35 years ago.'* He may have been safely delivered by Elizabeth herself.

Through her work in women's health she also came into contact with Margaret Byers and other leading campaigners for woman's suffrage. She, quite rightly, thought that it was ridiculous that she could be a Doctor but not a voter. Nowadays we are inclined to use the term Suffragette as a universal term to cover all those involved in the campaign for woman's suffrage. However there were two distinct wings to the campaign. The Suffragists were lead by Millicent Fawcett and were trying to win the hearts and minds of their male opponents through well crafted letters and arguments. The Suffragettes, led by the infamous Mrs Pankhurst sought to win the vote through a well-aimed brick through a window. They were the paramilitary wing of the movement and launched a campaign of arson, vandalism and even planted a couple of bombs. Elizabeth was a Suffragette.

Her commitment to the cause lead to direct action while on a visit to London. On 21st Novemebr 1911 she was arrested for throwing stones through Swan and Edgar's Department Store's windows. She was sent to Holloway Women's Prison and kept in solitary confinement. It should be emphasised that in their early campaign of violence the Suffragettes were so anxious that no-one should be hurt through their vandalism that they tied a length of rope to the bricks that they were hurling through windows so that only the window was broken and the brick could be retrieved. However as the campaign became more militant so did their tactics. Arson, Acid attacks and even bombs became increasingly common. For those interested in this aspect of the campaign for female suffrage I suggest reading *Death in Ten Minutes* by Dr Fern Riddell.

Elizabeth became very friendly with the Pankhurst family and also Lady Balfour, a leading Suffragette. While her great-niece Dr Shelagh-Mary Rea in her article in the Ulster Medical Journal claims that this was her only act of civil disobedience, other sources including Gordon Lucy report that she was suspected of being involved in an attack on the General Post Office in Belfast in November 1912. Sir Edward Carson had announced that woman's suffrage would be granted by a provisional government in Belfast, however he reneged on this when the constitution was published in September 1913. Gordon Lucy notes that *'this provided their justification for intensification of their campaign and, more specifically, their resort to arson against unionist-owned property. Dr Bell subsequently insisted that she checked there were no people in these buildings before they were torched.'* All of which would more than imply that her activities were quite hands-on.

In addition to her own activities she also offered her medical care for free to the Suffragettes who were imprisoned in the Crumlin Road Gaol. Many of these women went on hunger strike and were force-fed by the authorities, by placing tubes down either their throats or their noses. As news about the force used became known by the general public there was a general outcry, these were mainly middle and upper class women and so garnered more sympathy, so the government implemented the so-called Cat and Mouse policy whereby when a woman became incapacitated through starvation she was released from jail until she recovered sufficiently to be re-admitted to serve the rest of her sentence. By 1914 it was estimated that there were over 1000 active Suffragettes in Ulster. Dr

Rea reproduces the wording of the certificate Elizabeth was given in recognition of her services to the cause:

"To Elizabeth Bell

On behalf of all women who will win freedom by the bondage which you have endured for their sake, and dignity by the humiliation which you have gladly suffered for the uplifting of our sex, We, the members of the Women's Social and Political Union, herewith express our deep sense of admiration for your courage in enduring a long period of privation and solitary confinement in prison for the Votes for Women Cause, also our thanks to you for the great service that you have thereby rendered to the Woman's Movement. Inspired by your passion for freedom and right may we and the women who come after us be ever ready to follow your example of self-forgetfulness and self-conquest, ever ready to obey the call of duty and to answer to the appeal of the oppressed.

Signed on behalf of the Women's Social and Political Union,

E. Pankhurst E.Pethick Lawrence"

At the outbreak of the First World War most Suffragette and Suffragist activity ceased and members of both organisations were encouraged to through their efforts behind the war effort. In May 1916 Dr Louisa Altrich-Blake asked all the women on the Medical Register if they would consider joining the Royal Army Medical Corp. There was a snag, while they would be working alongside their male counterparts, doing the same work, unlike the male doctors the women were not given either military rank (all male doctors were automatically enlisted as officers) or status. However they were given the same pay, rations etc as temporary commissioned male officers, although they did not wear a uniform, which was only introduced in 1919.

Elizabeth was one of the first to answer the call and set sail for Malta on the 2nd August 1916, one of 22 'Lady Doctors'. Her salary was

24 shillings a day and she was contracted for one year. She served from August 1916 to July 1917 at St Andrew's Military Hospital in Malta, caring for injured soldiers from the campaigns in Gallipoli and other Mediterranean war zones. It was while she was there that she was reunited with Dr Isobel Tate, a fellow Queen's College graduate. Isobel Tate had a fascinating war campaign as a radiographer, working with a mobile x-ray unit in Serbia until in October 1915 she and the rest of her hospital unit had to retreat over the mountains of Montenegro and Albania, pursued by the Austrian and German army. Unfortunately Isobel had the bad taste to be born just over the county boundary in Portadown and so cannot be discussed in this book, however I would recommend putting her name into a search engine. Isobel and Elizabeth's reunion was to be tragically short-lived as Isobel died of the same disease as Elizabeth's husband, typhoid fever, on 28 January 1917 and was buried with full military honours on the 30 January 1917.

Elizabeth's son Hugo, who was educated at both Newry Intermediate School (presumably when his mother was incarcerated at Holloway) and Inst (RBAI), had followed both his parents into the Medical Faculty at what was now the Queen's University of Belfast at the tender age of 16. While at the University he joined the Officer Training Corps, and in November 1915 he joined the Royal Munster Fusiliers. He had to wait until he had reached the age of 18 before he could be posted overseas, which meant that he was ready to go to France in July 1916, just in time for the battle of the Somme. From July to November the 3rd Battle of Ypres, better known as Passchendaele, was raging just a few miles away from the ruined town of Ypres. Lieutenant Hugo Fisher was there for most of it. On 10th November he was injured and taken prisoner by the Germans. The regimental field diaries noted two reports of him having been hit in the stomach and lying face down in the mud, however when he wrote to his mother on 21st November he tried to play down his injuries and she told friends that *"he writes very badly that he is feverish and wounded in the left foot."* In fact he had large shrapnel wounds to his thighs and he died of his wounds on 23rd November 1917 at the age of 19 years, 8 months and 18 days.

The rest of Elizabeth's life was devoted to her medical practice. She continued to provide medical care to the Malone Midnight Mission and in 1919 was appointed as Medical Officer to Riddel Hall, which was a hall of residence for female students. Dr Rea records that

> *'Miss Duffin, first Warden of Riddel Hall said of Dr Bell, "she proved a firm friend and a rock of common-sense in her frank and friendly dealings with students' ailments and I much appreciated the way in which she told me what to note in various illnesses or note a student's general "type" or constitution".'*

She also became involved in the Babies' Clubs welfare scheme, which provided subsidised milk for impoverished mothers.

Elizabeth died on 9th July 1934 at her home at 4 College Gardens, Belfast. While there is a blue plaque for her at Daisy Hill Hospital, she has largely been forgotten. She deserves to be better known and celebrated.

LT-COL BLAIR MAYNE

DSO (3 BARS), CROIX DE GUERRE, LÉGION D'HONNEUR

1915-1955

Soldier and Sportsman

His outstanding athletic career was cut short with the advent of WWII. While serving in North Africa he was recruited by David Sterling as a founder member of the SAS, a regiment he would later command with distinction.

There is an old adage that 'a story's not worth telling if it is not well told' that is most apt when examining the generally accepted accounts of the life and exploits of one of the most decorated soldiers of the Second World War. The stories of the personal bravery, drinking binges, bar brawls, fights on rugby fields that accompany Blair Mayne abound and paint a picture of a superhuman individual. But how much of it is true?

I first began to question the received opinion of Paddy Mayne a number of years ago, when a family friend mentioned that he had belonged to the same Masonic Lodge as Mayne, so I asked him what he had actually been like. *"Very humble, good craic and quite shy"* came the surprising reply. What about his drinking? *"Well, of course he drank quite a lot, but no more than some others."* I was a little surprised as the stories that I had heard had him drinking in bars and getting involved in brawls, of him throwing grown men through bar windows. Shortly after this conversation Hamish Ross published his biography *Paddy Mayne: Lt Col Blair 'Paddy' Mayne, 1 SAS Regiment*. Ross had access to private family papers and Paddy's own journal, which had recently come to light, that previous biographers had either overlooked or not known about. The man who emerges from this biography is still brave, still slightly wild, but is certainly not the functioning alcoholic sociopath that is depicted elsewhere.

Robert Blair Mayne was the second youngest of four boys and three girls born to William and Margaret Mayne, of Mount Pleasant, Newtownards, Co. Down, on 11th January 1915. He had a secure, middleclass upbringing, at the tail end of a loving family. Margaret is often portrayed as being rather controlling, but then again she did have four sons and a husband who loved to practice target shooting on Sunday afternoons, so someone had to be in control. Much has been made of the fact that in the final years of his life Mayne tried to hide the extent of his drinking from his mother, with the predictable amateur psychological conclusions, however anyone familiar with the dynamics of the relationship between the Irish mother and her sons will not find it unusual. Paddy Mayne could face all that the Third Reich could throw at him without blinking, but he was not going to admit to his mother that he had spent the night drinking to excess.

The young Mayne proved himself to be a natural sportsman, team player and leader. He had superb hand-eye co-ordination and so excelled in Rugby and Cricket while at Regent House School, Newtownards, that he quickly secured his place on the 1st XV and 1st XI. In August 1936, while studying Law at the Queen's University of Belfast he won the Irish Universities' Heavyweight Boxing Championship and was beaten on points in the final of the British Universities' Heavyweight Championship. He possessed that elusive, but instantly recognizable trait of 'natural leadership' and was made captain of the Ards Rugby Club 1st XV at the age of 18 as well as Malone after the 1938 'Lions' tour. He won his first cap for Ireland in the Ireland v Wales match in April 1937. Several more caps followed in the next season and then in the summer of 1938 he was selected to play for the British and Irish 'Lions' Touring Team to South Africa. He played in all 3 tests and 17 out of the 20 provincial matches. One of the numerous myths about Mayne was that he was quick to indulge in what nowadays are described as 'unsanctioned acts of violence' or fisticuffs on the rugby pitch. However this is not backed up by the evidence of the extensive match reports that appeared in the press and certainly his conduct on the pitch did not arouse any criticism, whereas his skill did garner great praise. Certainly the behaviour of the visitors was no better or worse than previous touring sides and a lot better than the infamous tour of 1974. He played in every match in the 1938/39 international season when Ireland beat England and Scotland before being narrowly beaten by Wales. After the win over England on 11th February *The Northern Whig* wrote about Mayne's 'quiet, almost ruthless efficiency' as 'he covers the ground at an extraordinary speed for a man of his build, as many a three-quarter and full back have discovered.' There was a final match of the season between an Irish XV and the 1938 'Lions' in which Mayne sealed the victory for the 'Lions' by kicking a conversion in the final play of the match.

The game against Wales was the last time that Paddy was to pull on a green jersey as the outbreak of war in the late summer of 1939 took his life in a different direction, but one where his natural leadership and ability to work well in a team was to come to the fore.

He had joined the 5th Light Anti-Aircraft Battery Territorial Army unit in Newtownards on the 6th of March 1939 and reported for duty on 24th August. War was declared on the 1st September. On the 4th April 1940 Mayne was reassigned to the Royal Ulster Rifles in Ballymena. It was here that he met an old face from QUB's law faculty and rugby club, Eoin McGonigal.

Eoin McGonigal came from Co. Tyrone but had been educated at Clowgowes Wood College, Kildare, before matriculating in Law at QUB. He came from a family of lawyers. His father was a Judge, his oldest brother was a Senior Counsel in Dublin and another brother, who was awarded a Military Cross while serving in the Special Boat Service, Sir Ambrose McGonigal was a High Court Judge and Lord Justice of Appeal in Northern Ireland after the war. In some of the many articles and books about Mayne there is a suggestion that he disliked Catholics, although there is no evidence for this opinion other than the fact that he was an Ulster Protestant. Throughout his life he had many Catholic friends and he, like numerous Ulster Protestants up to the present day, was very proud to have donned the green shirt of Ireland. It is important to note that conversely Eoin and Ambrose joined the thousands of very brave men and women from what was then the Irish Free State who, recognizing that Nazism was a threat to world freedom, flocked north of the border or crossed the Irish Sea to join the fight to free Europe from oppression.

Although he was four years younger than Paddy, the two formed a firm friendship and spent most of their leave at each other's family homes. When Eoin was killed during the SAS's first mission in North Africa, Paddy spent his next leave searching in vain for Eoin's grave. He wrote to Mrs McGonigal apologizing for his failure to locate it.

The Commandos were Churchill's baby. Churchill, unusually for a politican had actually been a serving soldier and had fought in the First World War. Realising how perilous was the situation after the fall of the rest of Europe, he wanted a regiment of men to operate as guerrilla fighters in support of the mainstream regiments to 'butcher and bolt' disrupting German operations before they could become bedded in. Mayne and McGonigal were on secondment with the Cameron Scottish Rifles when they applied to join the new unit and were assigned to No 11 Commando and set sail for the Middle East on 31st January 1941. Ross says of this time that:-

> 'The idea of the Commandos strongly appead to him [Mayne] and suited his temperament … the year he spent in No 11 Commando was to be an important period in his military service: the training developed his potential and allowed the tactical genius that he was known for to begin to emerge.'

There was a great deal of opposition to the very idea of the Commandos amongst the high command and also other regiments, who complained that it attracted some of their best officers and men. This resulted in them being underused and led to frustration as Commando missions were cancelled or misdirected. It was during this time that there was one verified incident that helped to cement Mayne's reputation as a hell-rouser and is the foundation for all subsequent tall tales. While stationed on garrison duty on Cyprus (an important strategic, Mediterranean island) Mayne and McGonigal were drinking late into the night at a local bar. They were the last to leave and when they felt that their bill was too high Mayne forced the manager to stand on the dance floor while he emptied the contents of his revolver into the floor at his feet. He was placed on 48 hours open arrest for this incident.

Germany, supported by (occupied) French troops, was making advances in the Middle East and on 4 June 1941 11 Commando were sent to provide support for Australian forces in the Litani river operation. In command of No 7 Troop, Mayne personally stormed a French position, taking 40 prisoners, 2 machine guns and mortar. His Troop achieved their primary objective and by the time they succeeded in rejoining the Australians they had taken around 150 enemy combatants, destroyed communications and captured a small arsenal of weapons. The rest of the Commandos had not fared so well and the commanding officer, Lt Col Pedder, had been killed and they had lost up to a quarter of the company. 11 Commando were withdrawn and returned to garrison duty in Cyprus and Paddy was 'Mentioned in Dispatches'.

Pedder was replaced by Lt Col Geoffrey Keyes VC, who was the son of the Director of Combined Operations (1940-41) Admiral Keyes. Keyes was only 24 and had to work hard to earn the respect of his troops. He and Mayne did not get on with each other. Sir Thomas Macpherson (President of the Commando Association) who was in 11 Commando with both men recalled *'Blair thought him a little insincere and Geoffrey thought Blair a little unreliable, which was certainly not true because Blair was very reliable – he was merely eccentric ... and his troops thought the world of him.'*

Mayne didn't have to bother trying to establish a working relationship with Keyes as within a week he had left Cyprus, albeit under a cloud. The cloud is because of an incident that, over the years, has been exaggerated to outlandish proportions. According to Ross, Mayne and McGonigal were playing chess in the dining room when Keyes approached them. Words passed and Mayne stood up and pushed Keyes, who fell over cutting his eye on the side of a table. Mayne did not strike him. He did not knock him unconscious with one blow. He did not pick him up with one arm and throw him across the room. Nor did Keyes put him under arrest. Instead Mayne left Cyprus for Egypt, where he fell seriously ill with Malaria and was admitted to No19 General Hospital and then moved to a convalescent hospital where he remained between 13-27 July 1941.

Meanwhile, David Stirling of No 8 Commando had conceived the idea of refining and reducing the number of Commandos to enhance their effectiveness and enable them to operate in small, highly trained groups behind enemy lines, frustrating communications and destroying arsenals, aircraft and equipment. Stirling discussed his idea with fellow Commando Colonel Laycock as he had no combat experience himself and as Ross says:-

> *... needed someone who had proven himself a highly competent troop commander in action'. He was on the lookout for a certain type of soldier: very fit, very strong and very brave. Laycock knew just the person to fit the bill – Blair Mayne.*

Mayne's exploits in 1 SAS have filled many books and there are plenty of military historians better placed than myself to discuss them in great detail. Instead I propose to look at just the ones for which he was awarded his Distinguished Service Order (DSO) medals. Two of these were the subject of much myth-making in later years.

The first is the attack on the airfield in North Africa. The generally accepted version of this is that Mayne, crazed with grief over the death of McGonigal, walked into the Mess of an Axis airfield and opened up with a submachine gun, killing all the occupants before blowing up all the aircraft. So, how much of this is true?

At the beginning of December 1941, and following the abortive first missions in mid November during which McGonigal had been killed at Gazala, Mayne accompanied by five men and Mike Sadler, a Rhodesian and member of the Long Range Desert Group, attacked an enemy airfield at Tamet, 500 miles behind the front line. All six men returned uninjured. During the raid, and according to the report written by Mayne himself, 14 aircraft were blown up; 10 aircraft destroyed by sabotage; Bomb and petrol dumps blown up; Telegraph poles destroyed and '... *some Italians were followed and the house they came out of was attacked by machine gun and pistol fire, bombs being placed on and around it. The inhabitants there appeared to be roughly thirty. Damage inflicted unknown.*' In the section on any other remarks he noted that '*Guards were slack and when alarmed wasted many rounds in misdirected fire.*'

The Paddy Mayne Diary held in the SAS Regimental Museum includes a couple of newspaper cuttings, which may be regarded as 'Ground Zero' of all the subsequent embellishments. They appeared a few days after the event and were based on a press release issued by Stirling. One reads:

A British lieutenant, a famous international sporting figure before the war, walked into the mess with one man. They pushed the door open and pressed the triggers of their Tommy guns. It was all over in a minute. He threw a time bomb on the roof of the mess. Then on to the next job.

On 24 December Mayne and his men returned to Tamet, this time destroying 27 aircraft. In little over a fortnight he and his men had destroyed over 50 enemy aircraft. Mayne was promoted to Captain and won his first DSO.

Stirling was captured by the Germans in January 1943 and the decision was taken to split the SAS into two sections: The Special Boat Section and the Special Raiding Squadron. Mayne was placed in command of the SRS. Had he been the unstable character portrayed in some circles it is highly unlikely that he would have been given this command. Instead, it is more likely that his own proven coolness and effectiveness in combat, his leadership and team-building and his meticulous planning recommended him for the role. Unlike other regiments where the commanders orchestrated the missions from behind the front line, the SAS squadrons were led by their commanders into battle. Nowhere was this better illustrated than during Operation Husky on Sicily in July 1943, where Mayne won his second DSO.

Following the defeat of the *Afrika Korps* and Rommel in North Africa, the Allies were eager to open a new front in Italy, but first they had to take Sicily. In advance of an invasion the SRS were sent in to take control of strategic costal defences. To achieve this, on 10th July, they were landed from Royal Navy ships (one of which was, aptly, HMS Ulster Monarch) on a beach in the south-east of the island in daylight. Mayne's orders were to take the first objective and then to proceed as he saw fit. By the end of 12th July, Mayne and his men had captured and destroyed three coastal batteries, partially destroyed a fourth and killed or wounded over 200 enemy soldiers and well as taking around 450 prisoners.

The citation for his second DSO reads:

> '… *it was Major Mayne's courage, determination and superb leadership which proved the key to success. He personally led his men from the landing craft in the face of heavy machine gun fire and … mortar fire. By these actions he succeeded in forcing his way to ground where it was possible to form up and sum up the enemy's defences.*'

As the Allies progressed up through Italy, Mayne and the SRS were involved in several successful missions and, following the D-Day Landings, they played a key part in the fight to Liberate Europe. On 7 January 1944 Mayne was promoted to Lieutenant Colonel and appointed head of 1SAS with the authority to create five squadrons. Over the next few months he concentrated on finding and training suitable candidates. He knew exactly what sort of man the regiment needed. Fraser McLusky, chaplain to 1SAS recalled in his memoirs that:

> '*he was a very big chap, 6 ft 2 inches and a broad build in proportion; enormously strong – he was a giant … But along with this great physical prowess, he was very discerning and quick-witted and sizing people up immediately. If he thought they would fit, he could not have been kinder to them; if he thought that they wouldn't fit, they didn't stay for a minute.*'

He insisted that the men under his command were at the peak of physical fitness and trained them hard, but he also used his training in the law to anaylse all the field reports that were sent to him from agents and returning men so that his troops were as prepared as possible for everything that they might encounter, from how many enemy soldiers were in the area to questions about the reliability of equipment, including footwear. If any staff officers dared to question the behaviour or decisions taken by his men he was scathingly sarcastic in his written defense. One such unfortunate was Major Cliffe who earned the rebuke *'The statement that troops could have operated indefinitely unless their location was known to (the) enemy, is like saying the Army could march to Berlin unless something stopped them'.*

At this time British commanding officers were banned from infiltrating behind enemy lines but Mayne successfully argued that in his case this rule should be waived as he was commanding an extraordinary regiment and was the only person who had the necessary combat experience to make the appropriate assessment prior to a planned airborne landing close to Paris. This was at great personal risk as Hitler himself had ordered that any SAS personnel captured had to be immediately executed, a fate that befell Troopers Ion and Packman just days after he arrived. Accompanied by Mike Sadler he parachuted into France on 7th August 1944, his personal courage in the next few weeks led to his third DSO. The citation reads:

Lt Col R. B. Mayne DSO has commanded 1st SAS Regt throughout the period of operations in France. On 7th August 44 he was dropped to the "HOUNDSWORTH" base located west of Dijon in order to co-ordinate and take charge of all available detachments of his Regiment and co-ordinate their action with a major airborne landing which was then envisaged near Paris. He then proceeded in a jeep in daylight to motor to the "GAIN" base near Paris making the complete journey in one day. On the approach of Allied forces he passed through the lines in his jeep to contact the American forces and lead back through the lines his detachment of

20 jeeps landed for operation "WALLACE". During the next few weeks he successfully penetrated the German and American lines in a jeep on four occasions in order to lead parties of reinforcements. It was entirely due to Lt Col Mayne's fine leadership and example, and due to his utter disregard of danger that the unit was able to achieve such striking success.

And so to his last DSO. I feel that the best way to describe the actions that led to it is to quote the citation in full. The citation was for a Victoria Cross. It was endorsed by the very top combat command, including fellow Ulsterman and North African veteran Field Marshall Bernard Montgomery, however it was downgraded to a DSO. Even King George VI queried why he had not received the VC for his actions, but his sarcasm had obviously not made him many friends among the men who fought the good fight from behind a desk.

The citation reads:

On Monday April 9th 1945, Lt Col R B Mayne was ordered by the GOC 4th Canadian Armoured Division to lead his Regiment (then consisting of two armoured jeep squadrons) through the British lines and infiltrate through the German lines. His general axis of advance was N/East towards the city of Oldenburg, with the special task of clearing a path for the Canadian armoured cars and tanks, and also causing alarm and disorganisation behind the enemy lines. As subsequent events proved the task of Lt Col Mayne's force was entirely and completely successful. This success however was solely due to the brilliant military leadership and cool calculating courage of Lt Col Mayne who, by a single act of supreme bravery drove the enemy from a strongly held key village thereby breaking the crust of the enemy defences in the whole of this sector. The following is a detailed account of the Lt Col's individual action which called for both unsurpassed heroism and cool clear-sighted military knowledge.

Lt Col Mayne on receiving a wireless message from the leading squadron reporting that it was heavily engaged by enemy fire and that the squadron commander had been killed immediately drove forward to the scene of the action. From the time of his arrival until the end of the action Lt Col Mayne was in full view of the enemy and exposed to fire from small arms, machine guns, sniper rifles and Panzerfausts. On arrival he summed up the situation in a matter of seconds and entered the nearest house alone and ensured the enemy here had either withdrawn or been killed. He then seized a Bren gun and magazines and single handedly fired burst after burst into a second house, killing or wounding the enemy there and also opened fire on the woods. He then ordered a jeep to come forward and take over his fire position before returning to the forward position where he disposed the men to the best advantage and ordered another jeep to come forward. He got into the jeep and with another officer as rear gunner drove forward past the position where the Squadron Commander had been killed a few minutes previously and continued to point a hundred yards ahead where a further section of jeeps were halted by intense and accurate enemy fire. This section had suffered casualties and wounded owing to the heavy enemy fire and the survivors were unable at that time to influence the action in any way until the arrival of Lt Col Mayne. The Lt Col continued along the road all the time engaging the enemy with fire from his own jeep. Having swept the whole area with close range fire he turned his jeep around and drove down the road again, still in full view of the enemy. By this time the enemy had suffered heavy casualties and had started to withdraw. Never the less they maintained intense fire on the road and it appeared almost impossible to extricate the wounded who were in a ditch near to the forward jeeps. Any attempt of rescuing these men under those conditions appeared virtually suicidal owing to the highly concentrated and accurate fire of the enemy. Though he fully realised the risk he was taking Lt Col Mayne turned his jeep round once more and returned to try and rescue these wounded. Then by superlative determination and displaying gallantry of the very highest degree and in the face of intense enemy machine gun fire he lifted the wounded one by one into the jeep, turned round and drove back to the main body. The entire enemy positions had been wiped out, the majority of the enemy having been killed or wounded leaving a very small percentage who were now in full retreat. The Squadron having suffered no further casualties were able to continue their advance and drive deeper behind the enemy to complete their task of sabotage and destruction of the enemy. Finally they reached a point 20 miles ahead of the advance guard of the advancing Canadian Division thus threatening the rear of the Germans who finally withdrew. From the time of the arrival of Lt Col Mayne his gallantry inspired all ranks. Not only did he save the lives of the wounded but he also completely defeated and destroyed the enemy.

Blair Mayne and his beloved 1 SAS saw out the remainder of the war in Norway. They thought that they would be deployed to the Far East where the war against Japan was still being fought but those at the top of the military had other ideas. The Commandos and SAS had always been Churchill's babies but were not widely supported or appreciated by the top command in the Army. The SAS was to be disbanded after the war and the men who had fought in the regiment either returned to their original regiments or thanked for their service and returned to civilian life.

Mayne himself could have returned to his legal practice in Northern Ireland but he and Mike Sadler heard about an Antarctic expedition that was looking for volunteers and signed a two-year contract to ease themselves back into non-military life. It was at the start of this that Mayne began the diary that resurfaced after his sister's death. Unfortunately problems with his back resulting in severe pain cut his Antarctic adventure short and so he returned, aged just 31 to the family home at Mount Pleasant, Newtownards and civilian life.

Many who returned from the war, outwardly untouched, found the transition back to civvy street difficult. How much more so must it have been for Paddy. He had seen more combat action and faced more danger in five years than most career soldiers would see in four times that amount. The army had learnt very few lessons from the legion of shell shocked men from the First World War and men like Paddy were just supposed to get on with life and be grateful that they had returned home when so many of their friends had been left behind in some foreign field.

Mayne was also one of the most famous 'personalities' from the war. From the first successful operation at Tamet the press had followed his career and, much to his embarrassment, he was feted on his return to civilian life. He was plagued by insomnia, regularly drinking into the night and surviving on two hours sleep. According to Ross, Mayne outlines in his diary his attempts to learn self-hypnosis to combat the constant insomnia and pain from his back. The constant back pain meant that he was unable to play or even watch any sport.

He was appointed Secretary to the Law Society of Northern Ireland and proved to be very successful in the role. However he never settled. To anesthetise himself from both his physical pain and the inevitable mental scars he began to drink to excess. Visits from and to former colleagues and driving at speed round the country roads of Co. Down in his beloved Riley roadster helped and with time he may have been able to rebuild his life. But he didn't have time. On the night of Tuesday 13th December 1955, after drinking at the house of a Masonic friend in Bangor, he drove his car into a stationary milk float on Mill Street, Newtownards. He died on impact. His funeral was the largest ever seen in the town and most of his old colleagues turned out to see him buried with full military honours and pay their respects to probably the greatest soldier of the second world war. The funeral service was conducted by Rev Fraser McLusky, MC, 1SAS.

I suppose it is only natural that so many myths should have grown up around him in the past 70 years. Even when it is stripped back to the bald statement of fact recorded in official documents his life is extraordinary. That one man could have achieved so much in just 40 short years seems to be the stuff of legend and yet it was true. But I feel that the myth making diminishes him. They have left people with the impression that he was a high functioning alcoholic psychopath when he wasn't. He was an incredibly brave, incredibly loyal, natural leader of men. In the course of the research for this book I watched a programme where his old colleagues were interviewed about him. The love and respect they had for him was obvious, even 50 years after his death. They had followed him into the jaws of death because they knew that he would lead them back out again, even if he had to carry them on his back. Fraser McLusky said of him

"It wasn't his legendary exploits alone or his signal disregard for his personal safety. It was all of those things together, plus a sense of this man's greatness. He was great in the quality of his compassion. He really cared for those under his command and never spared himself in their service".

OTTILIE PATTERSON
1932-2011
Singer

With her diminutive frame and huge voice, she was the
leading European blues singer in the 1950s and 60s. As lead
vocalist with the Chris Barber Jazz Band she was often the
headline act with artists such as Rod Stewart hoping
to get on the supporting bill.

It is not often that anyone from Comber merits large obituary
articles in all the main, broadsheet, newspapers, however when
the death of Ottilie Patterson from Comber was reported on 20th
June 2011, and despite the fact that she had not performed for
over two decades, *The Guardian, The Times, The Telegraph* and *The
Independent* all carried large obituaries about the 'only … white
female blues singer' Ottilie Patterson.

Ottilie was born in Comber in 1932 to Joseph and Juliette (Julija)
Jegers. Her father Joseph came from a long line of amateur musi-
cians and played the accordion. He worked at one time as a chauf-
feur for the Andrews family of Titanic fame. Her mother Juliette
was originally from Latvia. The story of how her parents met is,
according to the Comber History website, *'a wonderful story all on
its own.'* Her mother escaped from the Germans in 1915 and made
her way south, towards the then Ottoman Empire, where she met

and married her Irish soldier boy in Constantinople. The newly weds returned to Co. Down after the end of the war and set up home together in Comber. There their family was born, two boys John and Jim, and two girls Jessie and Ottilie.

Throughout her childhood Ottilie was surrounded by music. In the footnotes on her 1966 album *Ottilie's Irish Night* she recalls *"Christmases and happy Saturday evenings spent with my whole family, in the little white-washed County Down farmhouse of my grandfather – himself a skillful melodeonist and fifer."* She studied piano and attended Regent House School in Newtownards, before travelling up to Belfast to train as a teacher at the Belfast Art College. At the Belfast Art College she was a contemporary and friend of Basil Blackshaw, Michael Baird and Enda Young (mother of the author).

It was while at Art College that she first discovered the blues. Her lifelong friend George Boyd, who collaborated with her on her *Irish Nights* album, recalled that in the early 1950s:-

> *"A group of us, including Ottilie and her sister Jessie, would travel regularly to the Cavehill home of the late Gerry McQueen, who had a fantastic collection of jazz and blues records. Ottilie liked what she heard and her natural talent came through as a singer with bands (such as the Jimmy Compton Band) at venues such as Chalet D'Or and the Fiesta Ballroom, both in Belfast."*

In 1952 she teamed up with two Art College friends, Al Watt and Derek Martin to form The Muskrat Ramblers and so her life might have continued, working as an art teacher by day, a blues singer by night, had it not been for a chance encounter between George Boyd and Humphrey Littleton in the Picton Hall in Liverpool. George remembers that *"I mentioned Ottilie to Humphrey Littleton. However he didn't want a singer but suggested that she should try Chris Barber ... and the rest, as they say, is history."*

Ottilie travelled over to London for a holiday with a friend and went to see the Chris Barber band at a nightclub. Somehow she plucked up the courage to approach the band and asked if she could sing with them. Initially they were very dismissive but she waited until the show was over and, as the band were packing up their instruments, sat down at the piano and started to sing. That was the start of what was a fabulous career. It was also the start of a personal relationship with Chris Barber which resulted in a marriage that lasted from 1959 to 1983 and a friendship that lasted until her death.

In the obituary published in the *Independent* newspaper on 4 July 2011, Spencer Leigh says that *'Before Ottilie Patterson joined the Chris Barber Band in 1955 it was accepted that British Performers could not sing the blues effectively.'* Ottilie proved to be the exception to the rule. She had a very distinctive style, the passion and depth of tone of Bessie Smith, but the distinct diction of a classically trained soprano. Tony Davis of The Spinners recalled *"I went to the Bodega. Chris Barber was there with his band and sounded excellent and then this young girl came out. Ottilie Patterson was a little slip of a girl, so thin, but she had a huge voice, an incredible voice. She sang Bessie Smith songs and I have never heard anybody sing them better."*

Throughout the second half of the 1950s and throughout the 1960s Ottilie was one of the biggest names in the world of Jazz and the Blues. It is difficult for a modern audience to appreciate exactly what that means as both have, to a certain extent, been sidelined and now compete with a multitude of different musical genres. However in the 50s and 60s the likes of Chris Barber, Humphrey Littleton and Cleo Laine were considered to be mainstream popular musicans. For example at the 1965 fifth National Jazz and Blues Festival at Richmond it was Chris Barber and Ottilie Patterson who were the headline acts and Rod Stewart and the Animals were supporting artistes. Similarly at the 1966 festival at Windsor

Ottilie claimed the large type while Eric Clapton and The Who were thrilled to be sharing the same bill.

In 1962, at the height of her fame, she was invited to perform at the President Kennedy's Washington Jazz Festival, more than holding her own with some of the biggest names in Jazz and the Blues from both sides of the Atlantic. Some of her best known songs include *There'll Be A Hot Time In Old Town Tonight* (1959) and *Mama, He Treats Your Daughter Mean* (1962).

Then in 1963 she began to experience throat problems and in 1965 was told by her medical advisers to take a three month break from talking, let alone singing.

After this setback she seemed to lose the hunger for performing, although she did do the occasional concert and festival, she drew back from participating in the grueling 200+ tours that she had previously undertaken with Chris and the band. In 1969 she launched a solo album called *Spring Song*, which included the song *Please Accept My Apologies, Mrs Pankhurst*.

During the 1970s Ottilie's performances were becoming more and more rare due to ill-health and family commitments. At one stage she moved back to Northern Ireland and lived with her mother in both Drumhirk (Comber) and Ballycrochan (Bangor). However in 1979 she made a rare appearance at the Magnus Jazz Festival and proved that she still had the same sublime voice. A jazz critic said that:-

> *"Ottilie Patterson, the little lady with the big Bessie Smith voice, rescued the first night of the Magnus Records Jazz Festival at Wembley Conference Centre. In her first appearance in the United Kingdom for seven years she dominated the audience just as she did in the 50s and 60s, sometimes sombre and sometimes just plain gutsy. The Chris Barber Band, with whom she has been appearing on and off for two decades, gave her excellent backing."*

This proved to be one of the last public performances that she made, although she and Barber issued a live album in 1984 *Madame Blues and Dr Jazz* and a compilation album *Back In The Day* in 1988. She also performed in a few concert dates with the band in 1991, but effectively she had moved into semi-retirement by the time that she and Barber divorced in 1983.

Not much is known about Ottilie's final years, and that is because that is how she wanted it to be. She moved to Ayr in Scotland shortly after her divorce and lived quietly and alone, although still a much loved part of her own family. In his tribute, on the Chris Barber website, her friend John Service says that:-

> *"She pursued her love of classical music, practising the piano daily and she continued to paint and sketch. She was one of the first people I knew to have a computer and had an amazing command and dexterity with it. She was also fanatical about classic western movies and had a collection numbering hundreds of videos and DVDs. Throughout her health issues, Ottilie maintained her mischievous sense of humour and I remember on more than one occasion both of us being in a fit of giggles!"*

Her final 3 years were spent living in the Rozelle Holm Farm residential home in Ayr. Such was her zest for privacy that by the time the world learnt of her passing she was already buried in the family grave in Movilla Cemetery, Newtownards.

All that remains now to remind us of Ottilie is a blue plaque on the wall of 26 Carnesure Terrace in Comber and a raft of music videos available on YouTube to remind us of the white girl with the big voice who could sing the blues – and boy could she sing.

THOMAS ANDREWS
1873-1912

Ship Builder

The son of a long established Comber mill owning family,
he was chief designer of RMS Titanic and was the managing
director of the Harland and Wolf shipyard
where she was built.

He perished on the ship's fatal maiden voyage.

One of my earliest memories is of being taken to visit a friend[1] of my parents and of her showing me a photo of herself as a young girl, dressed in Edwardian pinafore and petticoats, standing on the rails of a ship. A rather handsome man was supporting her with his arm and they were both smiling at the camera. The ship was called *Titanic* and the handsome man was called Thomas Andrews. Sadly I have no idea what happened to the photograph but I, and the rest of the world, know what happened to Thomas Andrews and the *Titanic*.

A quick search of the internet will bring up numerous accounts of Thomas Andrews's life. Of necessity they are dominated by his

---

1   I have forgotten the lady's name, but she lived in Southwell Road in Bangor and her father had worked in the Drawing Office at Harland and Wolff. He had started his apprenticeship at the shipbuilders at the same time as Thomas Andrews and remained friends. The photograph was taken on the day of the launch of the ship. She also had photographs of the Titanic sailing out of Belfast Lough for the final time.

tragic death, and include some distortions that have occurred because of the popularity of the better known films. In an attempt to find the real Thomas Andrews I turned to a book that was written and published in the year of his death by Shan F. Bullock. *Thomas Andrews Shipbuilder* was written at the request of Sir Horace Plunkett and the author was given full access to the hundreds of letters of condolence that the family received 'from all sorts and conditions of men, ranging from a duke to a pauper in a workhouse'. The sense of loss and pain felt by all his family and friends portrayed in the book is raw and all consuming, however what emerges is a more rounded character than the rather drier accounts from later in the century. Obviously it was written as a tribute and so no-one was going to say that he was a boor and wife-beater (he wasn't), but what is very evident is the huge affection that everyone who ever met him had for him. He emerges as one of those individuals who was just a nice person. He treated everyone with respect, no matter who or what they were, and earned their love and respect in return.

Thomas was born into a prosperous Presbyterian family on 7th February 1873. He was the second of four sons and a daughter born to Thomas Andrews and his wife Eliza Pirrie. The Andrews family had lived in and influenced life in both Comber and Co. Down since the seventeenth century and owned the large Flax Spinning Mill in the town while Eliza was the sister of William Pirrie, later Lord Pirrie, the part-owner of the rapidly expanding shipbuilders Harland and Wolff. Although it was expected that the young Thomas would make his way into one of the two family businesses, as a child he was obsessed with building toy boats and acquired the nickname of the 'Admiral' – so perhaps even from a young age it was clear in which his interests would lie!

His mother recalled a *'healthy, energetic, bonny child (who) grew into a handsome, plucky and loveable boy'*. He and his older brother John were inseparable and spent their days exploring the countryside, riding their ponies and, in Thomas's case, tending to their hives of bees. At the age of 11 Thomas became a pupil at the Royal Academical Institution Belfast (INST), following in the footsteps of both his father and uncle, William Pirrie. Although he never struggled academically he was more interested in the sporting opportunities offered by the school and played on both the cricket and hockey teams. Cricket was to remain a life-long interest as was sailing and riding to hounds. A school friend summed up the schoolboy Andrews, '*Wherever he went Tom carried his own sunshine*'.

On the 1st May 1889, aged just 16, Thomas left school and started as a premium apprentice at the Harland and Wolff shipyard. In her biography of her great-grandfather[2], Susan Cunningham recreates the conditions under which most apprentices lived in the late nineteenth century and Thomas was no different. He was expected to live in a dormitory with his fellow apprentices. He was woken up at 4.50am and was expected to be at work in the Yard at 6am precisely. Breakfast was at 8am and then lunch at noon. The working day finished at 6pm. It was hard, physical work and being the owner's nephew did not earn him special treatment, if anything he had to prove his worth more so than other apprentices. They were being trained in all aspects of the yard and so he spent 3 months in the Joiner's shop followed by 1 month with the Cabinet Makers; 2 month with the Shipwrights; 2 months in the Main Store; another 5 months with the Shipwrights; 2 months in the Moulding Loft; 2 months with the Painters; 8 months with the Iron Shipwrights; 6 months with the Fitters; 3 months with the Patter makers; 8 months with the Smiths and the final 18 months of his 5 year apprenticeship in the Drawing Office.

---

2   *Sir Crawford McCullagh: Belfast's Dick Whittington* Susan B Cunningham, Ballyhay Books, Donaghadee, 2016

'It seemed his delight to make those around him happy. His was ever the friendly greeting and the warm handshake and kind disposition.'

Shipyard foreman

In addition to his 12 hours per day of hard labour he studied for professional qualifications in Machine and Freehand Drawing, Applied Mechanics and The Theory of Naval Architecture, before collapsing into bed by 11pm.

In 1894 Thomas was 21 years old and ready to start his professional career. He stood almost 6 feet tall and was blessed with good looks and an easy manner. Many of the letters of condolence mentioned his booming laugh and good humour. His promotion within the company was rapid, but everyone from the shop floor up acknowledged that it was hard earned. He started in the Repair Department and moved on to become Manager of Construction Works for the building of *Celtic*, which was a huge responsibility. He had to supervise all the structural details of the vessel and had to co-ordinate with the Drawing Office, Moulding loft, Plater's shops etc as well as the owners, directors, contractors and managers. He was only 26. By 1904 he was promoted to become the Assistant Chief Designer. He became Head of the Designing Department in 1905 under his uncle Pirrie and in 1907 was appointed Managing Director, on top of rather than instead of all his other responsibilities.

'One sees him, big and strong, a paint-smeared bowler hat on his grown, grease on his boots and the pockets of his blue jacket stuffed with plans making his daily rounds of the Yards. He has been at the Yard since 4 or 5 am – since 6 for a certainty. At 7 or so he will trudge home, or ride in a tramcar with the other workers, to sit over his plans or his books well into the night.'

Lord Pirrie

In 1908 Thomas married Helen Reilly Barbour, the youngest daughter of John Doherty Barbour, and set up home in Dunallen, Windsor Avenue, Belfast. Their only child, Elizabeth Law Barbour Andrews, was born in 1910. Helen Andrews told a story about Thomas that is very revealing and explains his attitude to those under his management.

> 'One evening my husband and I were in the vicinity of Queen's Island, and noticing a long line of men going home from work, he turned to me and said "There go my pals, Nellie." I can never forget the tome in his voice as he said that, it was as though the men were as dear to him as his own brothers. Afterwards ... I reminded him of the words and he said, "Yes, and they are real pals too."'

Bullock's book is littered with examples, gleaned from the letters of condolence, of his kindness and commitment to the ordinary men in the shipyard. The early years of the twentieth century was time of political unrest and the shipyards were not immune to sectarian trouble. Andrews, at risk of personal injury, stood between his Catholic employees and those who sought to do them damage. Another ordinary worker recalled an incident when, in a gale, he climbed an eighty foot staging, rescued the terrified man who had gone up to secure the loose boards and then completed the work himself.

Unsurprisingly Thomas was interested in national politics, despite turning down numerous requests to put himself forward for election to the Belfast City Council, and he was a pragmatic, rather than an emotional, Unionist. He felt that Ireland did not have a sufficiently developed industrial economic base to be able to succeed independently and so would be better remaining part of the Union. He felt that a country dependent solely on agriculture was like a man fighting the battle of life with one hand. He approved of Sir Horace Plunkett's proposals for agricultural reforms (Co-operative societies being a major plank) and felt that if it was com-

bined with industrial development throughout Ireland that emigration would cease and that Ireland, as a whole, would become
more prosperous.

He was very interested in Labour relations and felt that one prime
means towards improving the conditions of the working class
would be for the State, either directly or indirectly through local
authorities, to provide them with decent housing. He held rather
progressive ideas. For example he felt that it was in the interest of
both workers and employers that the labour force should be organized under capable leaders. He felt that labour relations worked
best without outside political interference and despised those who
sought to foster class hatreds while never having held a labouring
job themselves. Some of his proposals were far in advance of his
peers. He thought that where economically possible the working
day should be shorter – he knew from personal experience what it
was like to do a hard, physical job for 12 hours a day. He thought,
again where economically possible, that the workforce should share
in the profits generated by their hard work. And he promoted the
idea that manual skills, essential to the production line, should be
backed up by technical educational qualifications. Is it any wonder
that in the words of one writer of condolence *'It was not a case of
liking him, we all loved him.'*?

Construction of the *Titanic* started in 1909 along side her sister
ship the *Olympic*. They were commissioned by the White Star
Line for the lucrative cross Atlantic trade and were designed, from
the start to be the height of luxury and modernity. There were to
be Lifts, Turkish Baths, Squash Courts and salt-water swimming
pools. Unfortunately, Andrews's wish to include more lifeboats was
over-ruled by those higher up than himself.

Bullock's book says of the ship that:

> *'Probably no one man was solely responsible for the beautiful thing.
> She was an evolution rather than a creation. As Chief Designer and*

Naval Architect he planned her complete. As Managing Director he saw her grow up, frame by frame, plate by plate, day after day, throughout more than 2 years. For Andrews this was his ship.'

Titanic sailed out of Belfast Lough for the last time in the evening of Tuesday, 2nd April, 1912. On board, in addition to Thomas Andrews, were 8 other men who would never return to friends and family. They were William Henry Marsh Parr, Assistant Manager Electrical Department; Roderick Chisholm, Ship's Draughtsman; Anthony W Frost, Outside Foreman Engineer; William Campbell, Joiner Apprentice; Alfred Fleming Cunningham, Fitter Apprentice; Frank Parkes, Plumber Apprentice; and Ennis Hastings Watson, Electrician Apprentice.

During the voyage to Southampton and in the days before she set sail for her first and final trip, Andrews and his team worked ceaselessly identifying and correcting minor defects. Nothing was too small for his attention and one of the last reports that he sent back to Belfast included a recommendation to reduce the number of screws in the hat hooks in the staterooms. His secretary Mr Thompson Hamilton, who had accompanied him as far as Southampton recorded that *'He would put himself in place such things as racks, tables, chairs, berth ladders, electric fans, saving that except he saw everything right he could not be satisfied.'*

Even after the ship left Queenstown (Cobh) his attention to detail was relentless. Henry E. Etches, his personal steward on board said that he went about the boat all day with his workmen, putting things right and making note of every suggestion of an imperfection. He then spent the evenings, after dinner, in his stateroom making calculations and drawings for future use.

There are many first hand accounts of Andrews on board the *Titanic* but there is one which I think sums up his character more than all the stories of acts of bravery and dedication to duty. Henry Etches recorded that after dinner on the final night *'he went aft to thank the baker for some special bread he had made for him; then went back to his stateroom'* where he changed into his working clothes. Andrews really saw everyone on board the liner as his equal and equally deserving of praise and gratitude.

Miss May Sloan from Belfast who was a stewardess on board and one of the last to leave the ship, due to Andrews insisting that she get on to the last lifeboat, talked of her chats with him when he talked about his family. Of the final night she says *'I saw him go into dinner, he was in good spirits, and I thought he looked splendid.'*

Much has been written about Thomas Andrews's final hours, how he was summoned by the Captain to ascertain the true extent of the damage; how he ordered an immediate evacuation of the women and children; how he went down below deck to try to assist to keep the boilers and electricity going for as long as possible to give the passengers the best chance of evacuation; how he personally assisted a woman to put on her life jacket and assisted her on to a lifeboat; how he reminded the male passengers that *"You are British. It is women and children first"*; how, when all hope was lost, he was seen on the deck frantically throwing deckchairs overboard to provide something to cling to for the poor souls in the water. He made no attempt to save himself.

In the immediate aftermath of the disaster, thousands of words were written in tribute to Thomas Andrews but perhaps the most sincere expression of loss was that witnessed in the Yard that he loved as the big, rough, working men stood bareheaded and openly wept for the loss of the man they were proud to call 'Our pal Tommy.'

FRANK PANTRIDGE

CBE, MC, MD

1916-2004

Cardiologist and Inventor

Pantridge's concept of initially treating cardiac emergencies on site rather than taking them to hospital first and his development of portable defibrillators to allow this has revolutionised emergency care throughout the world and saved countless lives.

When a true genius appears in the world you may know him by this sign, that the dunces are all in confederacy against him

Jonathan Swift

James Frank Pantridge was born, on 3rd October 1916, 'within mortar range of the spot where the Anglo-Irish Agreement was signed' at his family farm just outside Hillsborough. His individuality and scant regard for authority was apparent from an early age and it was suggested that he should leave his preparatory boarding school and attend the local primary school before advancing to secondary education at Friends' School, Lisburn.

In his autobiography, *An Unquiet Life: Memoirs of a physician and cardiologist,* he names the village doctor, Dr Boyd, as his inspiration to pursue a career in medicine and explains that *'Landowners, particularly small landowners, had a habit of directing one of their male offspring into a profession – the church, law or medicine. I was certainly not the clerical type and from an early age I had shown scant respect for the law so I was directed into medicine.'*

He entered the medical faculty of the Queen's University, Belfast, in 1934 where he was taught zoology (then part of the medical curriculum) by Professor T. Thompson Flynn, father of the actor Errol Flynn.

Half way through his first year he was misdiagnosed with Diptheria by a doctor, who did not even examine him. This meant that he missed most of the summer term before he was, eventually, correctly diagnosed with 'heart block'. The experience had a profound effect upon him. As he said himself *'The year 1935 changed my attitude to medicine ... I decided that if I were going to continue in medicine I would become competent and I would learn to deal with patients in a proper way.'*

He was true to his word. While young doctors and medical students invariably found him terrifying, his colleagues found him exacting and exasperating and officials found him contemptuously dismissive, his patients, especially the children, were invariably impressed by his warmth, his genuine concern and his willingness to listen to them and to take the time to address their fears. He explained his approach. *'I constantly impressed on my registrars and junior consultants the need to communicate with patients. A patient was not concerned about his chest X-ray, ECG or electrolyte data. What he really wanted to know was whether he was going to survive ... Very occasionally a patient would ask if he was going to die. I would say 'Yes. And so am I. But I don't know when either of these events is going to happen.'*

On 1st August 1939 Pantridge became a house physician at the Royal Victoria Hospital. 34 days later, on 3rd September, war was declared and the next day he and four of his colleagues signed up to the Royal Army Medical Corps (RAMC) although it was not until April 1940 that they were eventually called up. In total 13 of Pantridge's year of medical students were to enlist.

Pantridge was drafted to Singapore, attached to the 2nd Gordon Highlanders, and his experiences there were to have a long lasting emotional and physical effect upon him.

Singapore was considered to be the jewel in the Empire. Situated on an island it should have been impregnable and the fact that it fell, almost without a fight, to the Japanese could be laid firmly at the feet of the complacent and incompetent authorities, political, administrative and military. But most of all, Pantridge blamed Winston Churchill. He felt that Churchill had sacrificed Singapore to concentrate on the war in Europe. Just one aircraft carrier, or one tenth of the planes he sent to help Stalin, would have been enough to save Singapore. He decried the incompetence and complacency of the military and political leadership that led to the landward side of the island being largely undefended. In his autobiography he gives a vivid account of the horrors of the attack and defense. As a medical officer he was trying to save the lives of as many of the injured as possible. He already knew that the Japanese Imperial Guard had beheaded 200 wounded Australian and Indian soldiers and says *'I ensured that as many wounded as possible were moved back quickly and that those who could not be moved would never suffer at Japanese hands.'* He also gives one particularly vivid account of *'One Indian officer [who] came in with a hand on either side of his head. He explained that his head was about to fall off. A massive gash from a Japanese sword had severed all the muscles of the back of the neck down to the spine.'*

As a result of his fearless and ceaseless dedication to duty he won an immediate award of the Military Cross in the field. The citation for the Military Cross reads

> *'During the operations in Jahore and Singapore ... as medical officer attached to the 2nd Gordon Highlanders, this officer worked*

unceasingly under the most adverse conditions of continuous bomb-
ing and shelling and was an inspiring example to all with whom
he came into contact. He was absolutely cool under the heaviest fire
and completely regardless of his own personal safety at all times.'

With the fall of Singapore Pantridge was taken prisoner by the Japanese and spent 'The Endless Years,' as he called his time as a Prisoner of War, working as slave labour on the infamous Burma railway. These years left him with long lasting health problems and an enduring hatred of the Japanese. In his autobiography he re-counts numerous sanctioned acts of torture and cruelty, although some of his worst recollections were omitted. Disease was rife and the starvation diet meant that the death rate was huge and unre-lenting. Pantridge survived by boiling all water and over-boiling the meager rice rations. This may have helped him avoid both Cholera and Dysentery but resulted in him contracting cardiac Beriberi the condition to which he attributed his life long hypertension. Caused by Vitamin B1 deficiency, Beriberi causes the victim to become bloated and there is frequently loss of neural responses in ankle and knee. Cardiac beriberi is associated with enlargement of the heart and high output cardiac failure.

The prisoners were moved from one work camp to another and forced to work as slave labour, hacking a path through dense jun-gle and in monsoon conditions. The loss of life was immense and incomprehensible. A camp near Nikki, Sonkurai, two miles south of the Three Pagodas Pass was one of the worst. Of 1,600 British prisoners in that camp, some 1,200 were dead in eight months. Only 182 were alive at the end of the war.'

Towards the end of 1944, and in a very weakened state Pantridge was transferred back to Singapore and after a few months in Selerang hospital he insisted that he was well enough to work in the hospital in the notorious Changi jail. It was here, after the lib-eration of Singapore that he was discovered by his old friend and colleague from Belfast, Dr Tom Milliken. In the introduction to Pantridge's autobiography Dr Milliken remembers

> *'I found Pantridge in one of the many huts ... Pantridge said "Hello, Tom," in an offhand casual manner. The upper part of his body was emaciated, skin and bones. The lower half was bloated with the dropsy of beriberi. The most striking thing were the blue eyes that blazed with defiance. He was a physical wreck but his spirit was obviously unbroken. The eyes said it was indestructible ... He weighed just under 5 stones.'*

When Pantridge eventually returned to 'God's own country', as he always referred to his homeland, he set about trying to rebuild his medical career. After he completed his house physician's job, which had to be completed to progress in a career in medicine, he tried to go into general practice but a lack of vacancies resulted in him taking a part-time supernumerary lectureship in pathology at £150 per year. Dr Mary McGovern first met him at this time and remembers a withdrawn, monosyllabic man. Pantridge described himself as *farouche*, sullen or shy in company. She suggests that his experiences in the Far East had left him with a *'contempt, frequently ill-concealed, for those in authority or indeed for anyone in a position to made decisions that might affect him. It may have led him to question the textbook gospel and the merit of certain established medical practices.'*

Not unsurprisingly he decided to research the mechanism of sudden death from cardiac beriberi, and being Pantridge, did so by bringing pigs into the hospital laboratory – which caused not a little comment and a lot of consternation from the powers that be. However it was his work in this field that resulted in him being offered a scholarship for a year to the University of Michigan to work with Frank Wilson, the world authority on electrocardiography. He was in America for the 1948 Presidential campaign and recorded that *'I was delighted with Truman's victory. After all, Truman and the atomic bomb had saved my life.'*

Inspired by the advances in cardiac care he had witnessed in America Pantridge returned to the Royal Victoria Hospital, inspired to bring these advances to Belfast and the newly established National Health Service. In 1951 he established a cardiac unit in the RVH, with just 6 patients. By 1971 the unit had expanded to 80 patients.

Statistics showed that in the mid 1960s over half of premature deaths were due to ventricular defibrillation, i.e. the total disorganization of the heart rhythm. It had already been demonstrated by Kouwenhoven and his colleagues at John Hopkins Hospital that CPR and an electric shock or defibrillation could stop this, which was only useful if the attack happened when the patient was already in hospital, given the physical size and immobile nature of the equipment used at the time.

Pantridge argued that since two thirds of deaths occurred within one hour of the onset of the attack and therefore usually outside hospital, it would make sense to take the intensive hospital cardiac care directly to the patient. In 1966 he acquired an old ambulance and, together with his Registrar Dr John Geddes, equipped it with an ordinary hospital defibrillator, which they ran off a converted car battery to deliver the required AC current. The ambulance was staffed by junior doctors and cardiac nurses from the coronary care unit and a special telephone line was installed in the unit, which GPs were instructed to call if they suspected a heart attack.

The end of the cardiac ambulance's first year of service coincided with the annual general meeting of the Association of Physicians, which by happy chance was held in Belfast. Desmond Julian later commented:-

'It is difficult now to imagine the controversy that the introduction of coronary care created. Two notable figures in British medicine were vehemently opposed to coronary care – Geoffrey Rose, the leading British epidemiologist of the day and Archie Cochrane, the

arch guru of the randomized clinical trial. These individuals had a strong voice in the Department of Health, which discouraged developments in this area. So this was the china shop into which a bull called Frank Pantridge charged.'

It was to be 20 years before the Department of Health finally announced that cardiac ambulances should be available across the nation.

The response outside Britain was more enthusiastic. In America Pantridge is known as the 'Father of Emergency Medicine.' In 1987, Brian Maurer said that *'Frank Pantridge's name is known from Moscow to Washington and from Peking to Sydney. He could walk into any hospital in the world and will be instantly recognised.'* His achievement brought awards from around the world. He was elected to the fellowship of the American College of Cardiology in 1974. But from his own country – nothing. After being presented by a statuette of a guacho by the President of Uruguay he sent a postcard to a friend on which he had written *'I seem to be better known in South America that I am in Northern Ireland.'*

Desmond Julian points out that at the 1967 1st International Meeting on Coronary Care in Edinburgh attended by about 30 leading figures in the field. Three individuals stood out. Bernard Lown of Boston, Eugeny Chazov of Moscow and Frank Pantridge. Lown and Chazov went on to win a joint Nobel Peace Prize for their work on developing stationary defibrillators for use in hospital cardiac units. Pantridge didn't.

Most of my family work in medicine and often I would hear gleeful accounts of Pantridge's caustic wit at planning meetings, introduced after the reforms of the NHS that saw a massive growth in hospital administration staff. When asked by a leading London Cardiologist why patients in Belfast contacted their doctor within one hour of an attack while Londoners did not notify their doctors within eight hours. Were the Londoners more stoical? "No, more stupid." Came the reply. Alun Evans, writing in the British Medical Journal noted *'When Frank said "With all due respect" you knew that this was the last thing he meant.'*

One recurring themes of the stories I heard about Frank concerned his abiding hatred of the Japanese. One colleague told of how he was driving his new Japanese car home from the showroom. While stopped at the traffic lights outside Queens he was startled when the passenger door opened and Pantridge, glaring at him, said, "You are dead to me." He drove the car back to the showroom and said he had changed his mind. Nor where these stories confined to the medical community. Pantridge himself told the BBC that on learning that there were a group of Japanese businessmen staying at a hotel in Belfast he drove down just so that he could throw a pint of beer over them. However I also heard the stories about the atrocities he had witnessed, the casual violence and torture of fellow prisoners of war perpetrated by their Japanese captors. He had to live with the physical effects as well as the emotional effects of that treatment on a daily basis, so I think that he can be forgiven for a thrown pint of beer.

Outside of medicine he enjoyed playing golf and drinking good malt whiskey which was 'old enough to vote'. If he liked you he was a wonderful, very loyal friend and delightful company. An attempt to kidnap him by the IRA was foiled by his quick thinking housekeeper and thereafter he kept a loaded pistol under the driving seat of his car. Following the assassination of Lord Mountbatton in August 1979 he was requested to go to attend to the survivors of the bomb blast.

So why didn't he receive the official recognition that he so richly deserved? While it may seem harsh, it lies entirely at his own door. He made no effort to disguise the contempt that he had for petty bureaucrats and politicians. He did admire some officials, but they had to earn his respect. He was awarded a CBE but not the knighthood or peerage that his achievements deserved. Alun Evans said that his friends and colleagues did try to remedy this but 'Word filtered down from above that Pantridge was "controversial".' And how did 'God's own country' honour one of her finest sons? An airport named after him? No, but he did get a street in Poleglass called after him.

I have a personal reason to be grateful to Frank Pantridge as it was a portable defibrillator in the back of a Spanish ambulance that kept my three year old daughter alive until she could get to hospital. He also supervised the open heart surgery on my cousin when she was around the same age. I doubt that there is a family in Northern Ireland, or any country in the world that has not got a reason to thank Frank Pantridge for his vision and his gift to the world of cardiac medicine. The men who thought that he was too 'controversial' to honour will not even merit a footnote in history while the name of Frank Pantridge will be celebrated and honoured long after we are all gone.

> *"It was thanks to Professor Pantridge and his colleagues that in the late 1960s Belfast was often described as the safest place in the world to have a heart attack"*
>
> Irish Times 21/01/2005

> *"He was the giant on whose shoulders many of us stood."*
>
> Dr Denis Boyle (cardiologist)

> *"It is not often that one meets someone who really changes the world in which we live and work, but he was undoubtedly such a person."*
>
> Desmond Julian

> *"I owe him my life."*
>
> Barbara Drew, former patient

FREEMAN WILLS CROFT
1879-1957

Author

Although born in Dublin, he grew up in Gilford. He is
widely regarded as one of the leading authors just prior to
the Second World War in the golden age of crime fiction
with his popular character
Inspector French.

Freeman Wills Croft is largely forgotten nowadays, but at the height of his fame he was considered to be the foremost author of crime fiction during the so-called Golden Age of Murder.

I have long been a fan of crime fiction. This love was fostered at an early age by my great-uncle who was horrified to find me curled up with a Mills and Boons' romance and lent me his own copy of *Strong Poison* by Dorothy L. Sayers, which he assured me was one of the greatest love stories ever written. I was hooked at once and, although I will happily devour anything by local writers such as Colin Bateman and Ian Sansom, I have retained a great fondness for early twentieth century crime novels. I first became aware of Freeman Wills Croft a number of years ago when the algorithms of a certain on-line bookshop suggested *Sir John Magill's Last Journey (1930)* as something that I might like to purchase. Within the first few pages I was intrigued. The first hook was that the book was largely set in the newly formed Northern Ireland. The second was that the author clearly knew the country, and intimately so. Someone who has merely done a bit of groundwork research may have heard of York Street train station, but it is highly unlikely that they would ever have heard of either Whitehead or Ligoniel. And yet here were both places, correctly located geographically in the opening chapters of a novel first published in 1930. I determined to find out more about the author.

Freeman Wills Croft was born in 1879 in Dublin. His father, also called Freeman Wills Croft, had died on active service with the Medical Corps before his son was born and his mother married for a second time a Co. Down clergyman called Jonathan Harding, who was the vicar of Gilford. The young Freeman attended the local primary school before being sent to continue his education at Methodist College in Belfast. In 1894 he moved to the newly opened school Campbell College Belfast as one of the first intake of pupils, however he left at the age of 17 to take up an apprenticeship with his maternal uncle Berkeley Deane Wise, the celebrated Chief Engineer of the Belfast and Northern Counties Railway.

Freeman was obviously a talented engineering student and within three years had been appointed as Junior Assistant on the Londonderry to Strabane section of the Donegal Railway. In 1900 he was appointed District Engineer at Coleraine and it was here that he met his wife Mary Bellas Canning whose father was a local Bank Manager. They were married in 1912 and, while they did not have any children, they remained devoted to each other throughout their long marriage.

In 1919 Freeman was forced to spend most of the year in bed with a serious illness. I have been unable to confirm the nature of the illness, but in the days before the ready availability of antibiotics, many common illnesses could result in months in bed convalescing. It was during this time that he wrote his first novel, which was published in 1920, *The Cask.* This was the start of an impressive alternative career. Between 1920 and his death in 1957 Croft published roughly a book a year and in total had 34 novels, 3 short story collections, 2 stage plays, 1 radio play and 2 works of nonfiction published in his own name. In addition he collaborated in the Detection Club's 'round robin' mysteries, most notably *The Floating Admiral,* 1931.

Croft was a founder member of the Detection Club, which counted such luminaries as Agatha Christie, Dorothy L Sayers and G. K. Chesterton among its members. The fact that such a club existed (and still does) reflects the growth in the book reading public in the interwar years. This was largely down to the the growth in literacy among all classes of society due to the introduction of compulsory education in the last decades of the nineteenth and early twentieth centuries. Also there had been a rapid growth in the number of lending libraries in most major towns and cities that were free to join. By 1929 there were over 660 Carnegie Libraries in the UK and numerous other independent subscription libraries. While most were for the promotion of knowledge they had all moved with the times and stocked the latest offerings from a growing band of talented authors.

Among his peers Croft was very highly respected. Dorothy L Sayers was renowned for her often waspish reviews of fellow authors' books yet even she was moved to say that he was *'one of the most honest craftsmen in existence.'* He was one of the first crime writers to use a policeman as his main character and he eschewed the brilliance of Holmes for his creation and gave him what he himself described as a 'mere ordinary humdrum personality'. Before you reach for your keyboard or pen I know that the little Belgian with the abundance of little grey cells was a retired policeman, but Inspector French is still employed by a police force, rather than working as a consulting detective.

It could be argued that with his meticulous research about train timetables, the descriptions of bridges, boats, trains and automobiles that Croft brought an engineers' perspective to crime fiction. Not for Inspector French the brilliance of Holmes, or ingenuity of Poriot, or flights of fancy of the divine Lord Peter Wimsey. Instead as Croft said himself '*He does not leap to his conclusions by brilliant intuition*', instead '*when he gets the information he swots over it until he grinds out some sort of theory to account for the facts*'.

Such was the success of his creation and the proliferation and profitability of his novels that in 1929, at the age of 50, Croft decided to retire from engineering and he and his wife moved to Blackheath, near Guildford in Surrey, where he became a full time writer. It was around this time that he began to experiment with the form of the crime novel. He was by no means the first author to tell the story from the point of view of the murderer. In fact both Agatha Christie, *The Murder of Roger Ackroyd* (1926), and Dorothy L Sayers, *The Documents in the Case* (1930), had experimented with this style a number of years before Croft published *The 12.30 from Croydon* in 1934, however his was the first where the reader was almost persuaded to sympathise with the protagonist.

Given his background as a son of the Rectory, it is not surprising that there is a strong moral tone to many of his books, but not always in the manner that one might at first suppose. For example in *Antidote to Murder* (1938) he says that he is making 'an effort to tell the story of crime positively'. This inverted method of crime writing saw a greater emphasis on the character of the criminal rather than the method of detection. Many of his later novels reserve their real criticism for the greedy, the malicious but not always the culprit. His own faith and religious belief was explored in one of his non-fiction publications *The Four Gospels in one story* and he was actively involved in the Oxford Group of the 1930s and was an advocate for Moral Rearmament. In 1939, like his fellow countryman and county-man Sir Hans Sloane, he was elected to the Royal Society of Arts.

Croft continued to write until his death in 1957 at the age of 78. His stories faded from view in the intervening years as he was eclipsed by his female peers and more modern writers. Although, happily, many of the novels have been reprinted and/or recorded and are available in most good bookshops and online emporiums. Even when he was at the height of his fame, some criticized his 'hundrum' style with a lead character who was 'a home bird' who was happiest in 'his slippers before the fire', his nose buried 'in some novel of sea adventure.' However that is part of the appeal of Inspector French. He is a 'perfectly ordinary man … with the ordinary qualities of ordinary fairly successful men' who possesses 'thoroughness and perseverance as well as a reasonable amount of intelligence'. Given that they were written around 90 years ago, Croft's novels are surprisingly fresh and modern. They will not tax your brain too much, they will not give you nightmares, but you will be entertained, you will keep turning the pages and you will reach for the next one in the series. And after all, that is all that any crime novelist really cares about.

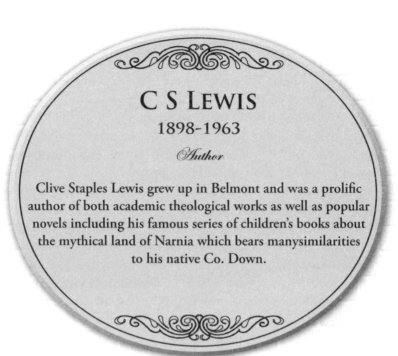

C S LEWIS

1898-1963

Author

Clive Staples Lewis grew up in Belmont and was a prolific author of both academic theological works as well as popular novels including his famous series of children's books about the mythical land of Narnia which bears manysimilarities to his native Co. Down.

Unlike most people my first introduction was not one of his Narnia books. Instead it was through a wonderful, science fiction book, we read in third form at school: *Out of the Silent Planet*, but I was reluctant to read any of the Narnia books. The main reason is that while at primary school I was told that Lewis was a friend of Tolkien and, as I hated *The Hobbit*, decided that anyone who could speak Elvish must be suspect. It was not until my own children were young and the first of the films based on the Narnia series was released that I, reluctantly, gave in to their demands to have the books read to them. I was immediately struck by how influenced the author had been by his home county of Down. The physical geography of the mythical land of Narnia is remarkably similar to the countryside of the county of his birth.

Clive Staples Lewis, also known as Jack, was born in Belfast in November 1898, the second son of Albert and Florence Lewis. His father was a solicitor and his mother was a graduate of the Royal University of Ireland (Belfast), so the house was full of books. By the time he was three he could read and he and his older brother Warren (Warnie) used to make up stories that bore the influence of the Beatrice Potter books, which had recently been published. Had it not been for events outside their control, he and his brother would have had a normal, middle class upbringing in their home on the Circular Road on the outskirts of Belfast. However when he was just 8 his mother started to become unwell. It was decided that Warnie should be sent away to boarding school in England and in 1908, shortly after his mother's death from cancer on 23rd August, Jack was enrolled at Wynard School, Watford. Given that in later life he would refer to the school as 'Belsen', it is safe to assume that this was not a happy time in his life. For a young boy whose mother had just died it would be difficult enough, but Wynard was ruled by a brutal, authoritarian headmaster who was already well on his way to insanity.

Fortunately his time there, although it must have seemed endless for him, was short and in September 1910 he was enrolled as a boarder at Campbell College, Belfast, less than a mile away from his Belmont home. Given that he was to spend almost all his adult life steeped in academia, Lewis had a troubled formal school-life. He never really settled anywhere. His time at Campbell College only lasted a matter of weeks before he was forced to withdraw due to severe respiratory difficulties. However we can assume that his short time at the school was tolerable, if not happy, as it was the only school he referred to by name in his autobiography. The decision to send him back to school in England was as much to do with the state of his health as his education. He was sent to Malvern, which was famous at the time as a health resort, especially for those with lung problems, and enrolled primarily at Cherbourg House before joining his brother Warnie at Malvern College. It was during this period of his life that he became an atheist.

Following yet more changes in scholastic establishments in 1917 the then 18-year-old Lewis was a student at University College, Oxford when he joined the Officer Training Corp before enlisting in the British Army. This is a moot point, which I have not been able to resolve. Lewis was an Ulsterman, albeit one who was at school in England, and there wasn't any conscription in Ireland. Therefore, it could be argued that he could have avoided military service. His older brother Warnie was already serving in France and by 1917 the harsh, brutal realities of trench warfare were already very well known, so his decision to enlist was an informed one and it is significant that he very rarely wrote or talked about his experiences despite having been injured on 15 April 1918 and invalided home.

In January 1919 Lewis returned to Oxford to complete his degree. He received a First in Honour Moderations (Greek and Latin Literature) in 1920, a First in Greats (Philosophy and Ancient History) in 1922 and a First in English in 1923. While still serving in the army Lewis had formed a great friendship with Paddy Moore who was killed in battle in the year of the war. It was during Lewis's second year at university that Paddy's mother, Jane, and sister Maureen, moved to Oxford. In 1921 Lewis moved in with them and remained linked to them for many years. However it was not Maureen with whom he had a romance, but rather Jane although he kept it secret for many years. In fact he and Jane and his brother Warnie, who retired from the army a couple of years later with the rank of Major, jointly purchased a house called The Kilns in 1930, with the two brothers only having a right of life tenancy to the property which was registered in the name of Mrs. Moore.

Lewis is probably best known nowadays as much for his theological writings as his children's novels. Certainly the *Screwtape Letters* is still relevant and accessible today. However for much of his early life he was a committed atheist and it was not until 1929, shortly before the death of his father Albert, that he became convinced that there was a God. As he recorded *'In the Trinity Term of 1929 I gave in and admitted that God was God and knelt and prayed.'* He told his friends that he was not yet a Christian, but rather a Theist: that is that he believed in the existence of a God and creator but was not committed to a particular form of religion. His conversion to Christianity followed in 1931. He had been discussing religion with friends such as J R R Tolkien but the actual conversion was sudden and occurred on an excursion to Whipsnade Zoo with his brother Warnie. In *Surprised by Joy* he recorded that *'When we set out I did not believe that Jesus was the Son of God, and when we reached the zoo I did.'*

In 1925 Lewis was elected a Fellow of Magdalen College, Oxford where he penned the Narnia books. As Lewis himself explained:-

> *The Lion all began with a picture of a Faun carrying an umbrella and parcels in a snowy wood. This picture had been in my mind since I was about sixteen. Then one day, when I was about forty, I said to myself: 'Let's try to make a story about it'.*

Although this would indicate that Lewis started work on *The Lion, the Witch and the Wardrobe* around 1939, the book was not published until 1950 by which time Lewis had finished a further three in the series, *Prince Caspian, The Voyage of the Dawn Treader* and *The Horse and His Boy* which were published over succeeding years.

He remained at Oxford for the next 29 years as a tutor of English literature and language, until moving to Magdalene College, Cambridge in 1954. He was everyone's idea of an eccentric Oxford don. His rooms were furnished with old, sagging chairs and there was always a glass of something to warm the soul on offer. He collected other eccentrics and academics across the University. The first meeting of the *Inklings*, a group of like-minded academics and literary professionals, met in Lewis's rooms in Magdalen College in 1933. For the next couple of decades it continued to meet, on average twice a week, and the members would read out their latest work to be critiqued by their friends. It was at this group that the dreaded Elvish was developed, but not to universal acclaim.

Having served in the trenches in the last years of the First World War Lewis was called upon to assist in the war effort in 1941 by giving a series of live radio talks on the BBC. The initial contract was for four broadcasts but they continued throughout the war and were on a religious theme. Some of them are still available on the Internet and one is struck by how English is his accent. However, should anyone have mistaken him for an Englishman he was quick to correct their mistake.

Lewis himself always thought of himself as an Irishman. He had ceased to live full-time in the country before the partition but he always maintained contact with the land of his birth. His holidays were spent in the same rented cottage in Cloughy every year and he kept in close contact with his childhood friends from Belmont. Lewis regularly spoke of Ireland as his 'home,' and drew inspiration in his writing from the countryside although he deplored the sectarian politics, north and south, of his homeland. Alister McGrath in *C. S. Lewis: A Life: Eccentric Genius, Reluctant Prophet* says:-

> *Ulster, he once confided to his diary, "is very beautiful and if only I could deport the Ulstermen and fill their land with a populace of my own choosing, I should ask for no better place to live in." In certain ways, Narnia can be seen as an imaginary and idealised Ulster, populated with creatures of Lewis's imagination, rather than Ulstermen.*

In April 1956 Lewis entered into a civil marriage with Joy Davidman, an American friend. The main purpose of the marriage was to give her British citizenship and thus halt her threatened deportation. However she was diagnosed with what was thought to be terminal cancer shortly after the ceremony and, in December, they were married according to the rites of the Church of England in a hospital room. Joy's cancer went in to remission and Lewis took her on a belated honeymoon in the Old Inn, Crawfordsburn in July 1958, to show her his beloved Co. Down. They enjoyed a couple of years of married life before Joy's death on 13 July 1960.

C S Lewis, Jack, died at 5.30pm on 22 November 1963 and what should have been a major event in the life of a nation was almost completely overlooked. At roughly the same time and a couple of thousand miles away in Texas, a young man walked into the book depository for the city library and shot dead the President of the United States of America.

Lewis's brother Warnie survived him by almost a decade and they are both buried in the churchyard of Holy Trinity Church, Oxford. Their father had kept their mother's calendar from the year she died and it had an inscription on it which both brothers wanted for their own epitaph.

Men must endure their going hence.

PATRICK BRONTË
1777 TO 1861
Father of the Brontë Sisters

Born and reared in a two room cottage in the Parish of
Drumballyroney near Rathfriland, through his hard
work and impressive intellect Brontë rose to study at
Cambridge before becoming an Anglican minister.

His daughters were literary giants,
the Brontë sisters.

*"I do not deny that I am somewhat eccentrick (sic). Had I been
numbered among the calm, sedate, concentric men of the world, I
should not have been as I now am, and I should, in all probability,
never have had such children as mine have been."*

Patrick Brontë to Mrs Gaskell 30 July 1857

If like me, your first introduction to the Brontë family was in a
twentieth century schoolroom then, if you know anything at all
about Patrick Brontë it will, in all likelihood, be due to his famous
daughters, and also not to his credit.

Patrick was one of a very exclusive group of early nineteenth century men who are better known for their famous daughters than
they are for their own exploits. He was in good company as others in the same boat included the Duke of Kent (Queen Victoria)
and the Rev. George Austen (father of Jane). However poor old

Patrick was the victim of a hatchet job by Mrs Elizabeth Gaskell (author and social reformer) of all people. Patrick had asked her to write a biography of his daughter, and Elizabeth's friend, Charlotte Brontë. Unfortunately one of the sources she relied upon was a village nurse from Haworth, who had been employed to look after Mrs Brontë in her final illness, but had been dismissed for drunkenness while on duty. In a gently chiding letter to Mrs Gaskell Patrick advised her that;

"It is dangerous, to give credence hastily, to informants – Some may tell the truth, whilst others, from various motives may greedily invent and propagate falsehoods."

Such was the hurt and outrage caused among the friends and family of both Patrick and his household servants that Mrs Gaskell had to make numerous corrections to the third edition; but by that time the damage was done and generations of children were taught that Patrick was a violent, taciturn, bad tempered man who forced his children to follow a virtually vegetarian diet, shredded silk gowns and was so hated by his own parishioners that he had to arm himself with a stout stick before venturing out of his rectory door.

During the latter half of the nineteenth century there were some attempts to rectify the damage to his reputation, not least by the Rev. Dr. William Wright, a Presbyterian Minister from Rathfriland, but it is only in recent years that serious progress has been made in examining his life and the influence he had on the writings of his famous offspring. As a result Brontë's reputation has been re-examined, revised and restored, thanks in large part to the efforts of Juliet Barker, *The Brontës,* (2010), Dudley Green, *Patrick Brontë: Father of Genius,* (2010), and to a lesser extent Samantha Ellis, *Take Courage: Anne Brontë and the Art of Life,* (2018). The man who emerges from their pages is far removed from the pistol firing at dawn monster described by Mrs Gaskell.

So who was Patrick Brontë? Well for a start he was not Brontë but rather Prunty. There is a theory that when he first tried to enroll at Cambridge University the admissions officer could not understand his thick Co. Down accent and made a stab at spelling the surname. Patrick obviously liked the spelling as it stuck and added the ë. This was not that unusual as spelling in general and that of surnames in particular was rather more fluid than it is nowadays[1].

Patrick was born on St Patrick's day 1777, the eldest of 10 children born to Hugh and Alice Prunty of Emdale in the parish of Drumballyroney, Co. Down. Patrick, in a letter to Mrs G, says that his father was originally from the south of Ireland and *"... his lot in life as well as mine depended, under providence, not on family descent but our own exertions"*.

Patrick was remarkably reticent about his early life although these years were eagerly examined by the Rev. Dr. Wright in the last decade of the century. However one is struck by a certain bias in his writings. In fact it could be argued that a suitable title for his book *The Brontës in Ireland (1893)* could be *How the Presbyterians influenced literary genius.*

The main benefit of Wright's research from our concern is that he was able to interview people who had known all the family members. One of Wrights sources was the Rev William McAllister who had known the family very well in his childhood. The Rev McAllister said that Hugh, Patrick's father, was a very well known storyteller who had often told a story about his own grandfather. Hugh's grandfather, a farmer on the banks of the Boyne, often travelled to Liverpool and on one occasion brought home an orphan boy that he had adopted. The boy was called Welsh and while a great favourite of the old man, was despised by every other member of the family. Eventually the old man died and the fam-

---

1   Having said that, anyone who reads the comments on social media could argue that, despite spell check being available on even the most basic of phones, tablets etc, we are rapidly returning to an earlier age in this respect!

ily threw Welsh out of the farm, but he returned a few years later with enough money to buy the farm from the family. He offered to adopt one of the children from the family so that eventually ownership of the farm would revert to the family, but was so tyrannical and harsh that the young boy ran away at the first opportunity and escaped to Co. Down. That young boy was Hugh Prunty.

Sound familiar? Of course by the time that the Rev. McAllister retold this tale of Hugh's to the Rev. Wright all the Brontë family were long gone and everyone had read *Wuthering Heights* but maybe Emily was using her grandfather's story as inspiration. This is not as far fetched as one might suspect. While a curate in Dewsbury in 1809-10, Patrick was leading a Sunday School parade when it was halted by a rather beligerant drunk, who would not get out of the way. W.W. Yates in his book *The father of the Brontës (1897)* interviewed several people who either witnessed the event or had heard about it from their parents. Mr Senior had been in the parade and described the drunk as *"a notorious cockfighter and boxer"* while Mr Wilson Hemingway's mother, who had been at the front of the parade often told her children how, when spectators could not persuade him to get out of the way *"the revd. Gentleman coming hastily up, flung him to the side of the road."* Many years later Charlotte Brontë used this as the inspiration for the scene in *Shirley* where Mr Helstone confronts the rival parade of dissenters.

According to the *Belfast Mercury* of April 1855 Hugh and Alice Prunty *'were of humble origin, but their large family were remarkable for their physical strength and person beauty.'* Theirs was a true romance as Alice eloped with Hugh on the actual day of her wedding to another man. They worked hard and managed to send their children to the local country school and while money was never abundant they did not starve. Wright recounts that the family possessed a few books including the poems of Robert Burns and *Paradise Lost* and it was a knowledge of this particular book that first brought Patrick to the attention of a local Presbyterian minister, Rev. Andrew Harshaw, who overheard this farm boy reciting Milton and was moved to offer to give him extra tuition. It was thanks to Rev. Harshaw that the 16 year old Patrick Prunty was made schoolmaster at Glascar Hill Presbyterian School and then, around 1797/98, schoolmaster at the Drumballyroney Parish school where he came under the influence and patronage of the Rev Thomas Tighe, the Church of Ireland Minister.

The date of his move to Drumballyroney school is very significant as this was the time of the rise and ultimate fall of a form of radical Irish nationalism that, at least in its truest form, was non-sectarian – namely the United Irishmen. Also County Down was one of the northern strongholds of the movement and when the rebellion broke out even Presbyterian ministers were involved in the battles at Saintfield and Ballynahinch. The Prunty family were not immune and one of Patrick's brothers, William, fought at the Battle of Ballynahinch (12-13 June 1798) before escaping to Co. Armagh and then returning home. William was fortunate in that he appears to have escaped the worst of the reprisals, which saw many men executed for their involvement in the rebellion, or transported to Australia.

There is no evidence that Patrick was involved in either the United Irishmen or the rebellion, on either side. However he retained a lifelong sympathy with those who sought to change their circumstances, so long as they remained within the law although he was vehemently pro Union. While a young curate in Yorkshire one of his parishes, Hartshead, was the scene of much Luddite activity. Patrick, alone among the clergy of the established church, did not condemn their actions. Yates in his book states that he turned a blind eye to midnight burials in his churchyard, which were probably those who had been killed in Luddite attacks. Similarly after the 1798 rebellion, the United Irishmen dead were often interred late at night in family graves, to avoid the attention, and subsequent retribution, of the authorities on the remaining family. While he did not condone the actions of the Luddites, Brontë's silence on the matter could, and perhaps should, be taken for sympathy.

The Rev. Harshaw and Rev. Tighe were the first of many men of influence who helped Patrick to advance from his start in life in a small, two room cottage in Co. Down. It was the Rev. Tighe who persuaded Patrick that he was capable of pursuing a university education and clerical career. Wright implied that the choice of the Church of England over the Presbyterian ministry was down to the fact that the former university course was shorter. And who is to say that he is wrong? As it was, the very idea of a small tenant farmer's son going to university, especially in the late eighteenth century was rather far fetched and, having nurtured the ambition, the problem of finance would have loomed very large in Patrick's mind. Unlike Hans Sloane a century earlier, Patrick did not have the backing of men with large pocket books. He was going to have to rely on his own ability to win scholarships and at this he was remarkably successful.

At this time there were three universities that provided training for the Anglican clergy. They were Oxford, Cambridge and Trinity College, Dublin. While one would imagine that Trinity would have been a natural choice, in effect Cambridge was the only one considered. St John's College was Rev Tighe's *alma mater* and it also provided financial support for poor but able men to attend university. In July 1802, at the age of 25, Patrick left his family and the land of his birth behind him to start on his university education.

Patrick entered St John's College as one of four Sizars. The position of sizar meant that he received a reduction in his fees and free board and lodging in return for some minor domestic service and having to record the names of those students who failed to attend the compulsory university sermon. Patrick arrived in Cambridge with just £10 in his pocket for his university admission fee. There after he had to pay 6s 4d each quarter so the donation from an anonymous (to us) friend of £5 would have been much appreciated. Patrick excelled at the university and with the exception of the first Christmas exams he was always listed in the first class of his year: only one of five to do so. This entitled him to win both university prizes (literary rather than monetary) and exhibitions. Dudley Green estimates that the exhibitions won by Patrick would have provided him with an annual income of between £6 to £7 per year throughout his time at Cambridge. While he was able to augment his income with tutoring other students, he made the decision quite early on in his university career to become ordained.

He approached a fellow of the college, Henry Martyn, a leading light in the evangelical wing of the Church of England, to ask him for advice and it was through Martyn that he came to the notice of one of the most famous men of the early nineteenth century, William Wilberforce. It was a case of a friend of a friend of a cousin, but the upshot was that William Wilberforce and his cousin Henry Thornton M.P., on the recommendation of Martyn, agreed to support Patrick financially for the rest of his time in Cambridge. A letter of thanks, dated 14th Feb 1804 is endorsed in Wilberforce's own hand *'Marytn abt Mr Bronte Henry & I to allow him 10L [£] each anny.'*

Nor was Wilberforce the only man of influence who Patrick impressed. He was a member of the Volunteer Militia at the college, which was led by a fellow student John Henry Temple who is better known to history as Lord Palmerston. Mrs Gaskell refers to this friendship *'I have heard him allude, in late years, to Lord Palmerston as one who had often been associated with him...'* However she does not elaborate on how he used this association – not for self-advancement but rather to save one less fortunate than himself.

While he was a young and new curate in Dewsbury he appealed to both Wilberforce and Palmerston to help one of his young parishioners, William Nowell of Daw Green who was accused and convicted of desertion from the army. There was just one problem with this – he had never enlisted. The magistrate who heard the case refused to admit all evidence that not only had he not enlisted but had not been at the fair where it was supposed to have taken place. Even when confronted by sworn statements from numerous witnesses, of good standing, to the effect that they had been with him or saw him miles away from the fair, the magistrate and authorities refused to admit that they had made a mistake. Patrick sent all the evidence to both Wilberforce and then Palmerston, after which the unfortunate Nowell was released and the enlisting officer was convicted of perjury and enjoyed an extended visit to the Antipodes.

At a time when it was who you knew, not what you knew that offered the most secure route to advancement in all professions, it is notable that Patrick does not appear to have tried to make use of any of his connections for personal advancement. He certainly impressed those who heard him preach, including in later years when he was blinded by cataracts and preached for precisely 30 minutes each Sunday with no notes, and was diligent in his pastoral care. However to advance in a profession that was top heavy with third sons of aristocrats, he would have needed a well-connected sponsor. And in Wilberforce he would have had one. And yet no evidence exists of any requests for help.

At the start of his ministry Patrick was drawn towards the evangelical wing of the church and most of his parishes, with the exception of a couple of years in Essex, were in the heart of dissenting Yorkshire where the majority of the parishioners were Methodists. Unlike most of his contemporaries within the Church of England, Patrick always got on very well with his Methodist neighbours. In fact,

Mrs Brontë was a Methodist. His close bond with Presbyterianism no doubt was a factor in this. In fact, when it came to his final appointment at Haworth his knowledge of Presbyterianism assisted him to secure the position.

Haworth came under the control of the Vicar of Bradford, who could appoint its curate. However, the Church Trustees were the ones who had to approve the appointment and pay the curate's wages. Over the years this anomaly led to something of a power struggle between vicars and trustees, each of whom viewed the other's candidate with suspicion. Patrick, by this time a married father of six, was the Vicar's candidate and so was going to be suspected by the Trustees. In an attempt to pre-empt any opposition he went to visit the Trustees, who assured him that it wasn't anything personal but that they were not going to select him, so he told the Vicar that he was withdrawing his candidacy. The Vicar, annoyed at having his will thwarted urged him to reconsider and when that didn't work went ahead and attempted to impose another curate on the reluctant parish. The situation descended into farce. In scenes that would not have disgraced the pages of Anthony Trollope's *Barchester Chronicles* for three successive weeks the new nominee tried to preach at Haworth as the parishioners stamped their clog-shod feet, hooted in derision, stationed a drunken chimney-sweep under the pulpit to repeat everything the curate said and, finally, rode a donkey round the inside of the church.

While this farce was playing itself out Patrick was quietly launching a charm offensive. Despite assuring everyone from the Archbishop of York down that he had withdrawn his candidacy, he invited the Trustees to come, unannounced to hear him preach. Not unlike the way in which the elders of a vacant congregation in the Presbyterian church will pay anonymous visits to suitable ministers before deciding to issue a call. Whether or not they did so his efforts paid off and on 8th February 1820 he was once again offered the curacy – but this time by not only the Vicar of Bradford, but also the Church Trustees. The family moved into the parsonage at Haworth in April 1820.

'I was at Haworth, a stranger in a strange land. It was under these circumstances after every earthly prop was removed, that I was called on to bear the weight of the greatest load of sorrows that ever pressed upon me.' So wrote Patrick to the Rev. John Buckworth on the 27th November 1821 after the death of his beloved wife. Poor Patrick if only he had known but his load of sorrows was only going to increase.

Patrick and Maria Branwell had met when he was a young curate in Hartshead, Yorkshire. She was originally from a prosperous family in Penzance, Cornwall and they first met when she was staying with her uncle who ran a school and Patrick was asked to come to act as an external examiner for the classics students. The pair exchanged love letters throughout their courtship although only a handful of hers remain. Patrick wrote her poems and she called him 'My dear saucy Pat.' They married on 29th December 1812 in a joint ceremony with his friend William Morgan and Maria's cousin Jane Fennell.

Maria and Patrick seemed to have enjoyed a very happy marriage and they were soon the proud parents to six children; five girls and a son Patrick Bramwell. Although according to Mrs Gaskell

> *"Mr Brontë … was not naturally fond of children, and felt their frequent appearance on the scene as a drag both on his wife's strength and as an interruption to the comfort of the household."*

Perhaps this was only natural in the eldest of ten siblings. Shortly after the move to Haworth it became apparent that his beloved Maria was dying of cancer. The eldest daughter, Maria, was only 7 and the youngest, Anne, was not even a year old. Patrick, without shirking any of his parochial duties, devoted himself to her care. Even the drunken old nurse who filled Mrs Gaskell's ears with bile could not bring herself to say otherwise *"Mrs Brontë was … devotedly fond of her husband, who warmly repaid her affection, and suffered no one else to take the night nursing."*

Patrick was devastated by his loss. He withdrew from the world, his family and his friends for two weeks, shutting himself away and giving in to his utter despair and loss. When he emerged he threw himself into the duties of his parish and trying to work out what to do with his young family. It was then that he made the disastrous decision to send his daughters away to Cowan Bridge school. This was not the act of an uncaring father. He had visited the school, was friends with the headmaster and had other friends whose daughters attended. Despite what Mrs Gaskell claims he did not send the younger children back after his two eldest daughters, Maria and Elizabeth, died from consumption/tyhoid fever. He was devastated by the loss of his two daughters and, it cannot be doubted, he blamed himself. Although he kept his remaining daughters at home, he could never be described as a 'helicopter' parent, allowing them a degree of independence, both physical and intellectual that was unusual in a father of that time and of their station. Even Mrs Gaskell admits that he encouraged his daughters to read the national and local newspapers in the house and to debate the leading issues of the day with him. He celebrated their intelligence and gave them the freedom in which to develop it. He took his young brood on long walks on the moors, took them with him when he visited neighbours, and even taught Emily how to shoot at targets. While he may not have known that they had written and published books when it came to his attention he was delighted and proud. At a time when most fathers became alarmed if their daughters read a novel, Patrick celebrated that fact that his daughters had written them. And what novels! Much as I love Jane Austen, the quiet villages of her novels are far removed from the descent into madness and violence of *Wuthering Heights* or *Jane Eyre*.

It is difficult not to feel some sympathy for and admiration of this quiet son of Down. He outlived his entire family by six years. He was in his own words *"somewhat eccentrick"* but he was never deliberately vicious. He used his influential connections to help others, not himself. He exercised a muscular form of Christianity, but was on good terms with those of all faiths and convictions. He struggled to support his only son, who was addicted to both opium and alcohol, paying his debts, trying to help him battle his demons, but never turning his back on him or turning him out of the house. Even after he had his reputation trashed by Mrs Gaskell in the first two editions of her book on Charlotte, he only asked for simple corrections and allowed some of the more critical passages to remain, as if attempting to see himself as others saw him.

As he said himself:

> *"Had I been numbered among the calm, sedate, concentric men of the world, I should not have been as I now am, and I should, in all probability, never have had such children as mine have been."*

And in that case we would all be so much the poorer.

MARGARET BYERS

1832-1912

Women's Education

The founder of Belfast's Victoria College, she ensured that
the girls in her care received a standard of education at
least the equal of that offered at the best male schools –
a revolutionary concept at the time which increased
education standards across the board.

I must declare an interest. I was educated at Victoria College.
My life has been shaped by the education I received, taught by
teachers many of whom themselves were Victorians, in a school
where the influence of Margaret Byers was still tangible throughout my years as a student. Therefore, it is impossible for me to take
a detached view of a woman who was, in my opinion, one of the
most influential Irish women of her day.

Margaret Byers (nee Morrow) was born in Rathfriland in 1832,
the youngest child and only daughter of Andrew Morrow and his
wife Margaret Herron. The Morrows were a relatively prosperous
family who also owned a Flax Mill to supplement their farming income. Margaret's parents were devout Presbyterians (her father was
an Elder) and Temperance Reformers – guiding principles with
which they imbued their young daughter and which she retained
throughout her long life.

When Margaret was eight years old Andrew Morrow died. Her mother, who had been almost 50 when Margaret was born, made the decision to send her daughter over to her paternal uncles in Stoke-on-Trent. Her uncles were prosperous businessmen in the rapidly developing town and sent their young charge to a Ladies College in Nottingham and it was while at this school that Margaret first embarked upon her teaching career having been inspired by the principal of the school to believe that 'Women can do anything under God'.

In February 1852, aged just 19, Margaret returned home briefly to marry the Rev. John Byers who, like her, came from a farming and flax family. John was inspired by missionary zeal and, under the auspices of the American Presbyterian Church missionary society, shortly after their wedding he and Margaret set out for Shanghai, China. Unfortunately, soon after the birth of their son John, her husband fell critically ill and the young family were recalled to America. John senior died just days before their boat arrived back to New York and Margaret, aged just 20 years old, had to make the hazardous and grueling journey home to Ireland alone. The fastest crossing of the Atlantic at this time was 10 days by steamship and the cheapest fare of £20 was too expensive for a young widow, so Margaret and John had to endure several weeks at sea, travelling steerage on a sailing ship.

Once safely back in Ireland, Margaret was determined to support both herself and her young son. She turned down the offer of a £20 p.a. pension offered by the Mission and, leaving John with relatives in Rathfriland, she secured a teaching job in Cookstown at a mediocre school for the daughters of local businessmen. She rarely spoke of this time in her life, and never with any affection. However it did inspire her to open up her own school and convinced her of the need to offer girls an education on a par with that on offer to their brothers, rather than lessons in embroidery, flower arranging and deportment.

Alison Jordan, in her excellent biography *Margaret Byers: pioneer of women's education and founder of Victoria College Belfast,* in a typically ascerbic turn of phrase states that:

> *"There was a great deal of wool-work parrots and roses in mid-nineteenth century women's education, and knowledge of arithmetic and English grammar was meager indeed."*

Certainly there was a requirement for improvement, but was there the desire?

Although she had no family living in Belfast Margaret did have a good deal of influential contacts and friends within the Presbyterian community in the city. Also the time was ripe for such a school. The 1850s saw the start of an unprecedented growth in the city, with the population growing from 120,000 in the 1861 census to 387,000 in 1911. This meant that there was a growing, prosperous and progressive middle-class, some of whom, surely, had daughters that they wished to educated beyond the drawing room.

To this end in 1859, aged just 27, Margaret opened an 'Establishment for the Boarding and Education of Young Ladies' at 15 Wellington Place. Her school was close to Royal Belfast Academical Institution (Inst) and her neighbours were professional and businessmen including Charles Lanyon, the celebrated architect, as residential Belfast was still clustered round the centre of the city.

Writing in the Victoria College Magazine of 1887 Margaret said that:

> *'My aim was to provide for girls and education adapted to their wants as thorough as that which is afforded to boys in schools of the highest order; in fact to work out for girls a practical and well-considered plan of education, in which due regard should be given*

to the solid branches of learning, as well as to moral and religious training.'

The first 35 pupils, (13 of them boarders) received instruction in Euclid (geometry), modern History, natural science, English grammar and mathematics, although the inclusion on the curriculum of handicrafts and other 'traditional' subjects meant that 'wool-work parrots and roses' were much in evidence too. In 1959, the then 98 year old Mrs Mary Jane Bruce, who was a pupil at the school from 1872 to '74, recalled her dancing classes with Dr Bruno with as much affection as the Current Affairs classes where she had discussed the latest machinations of Mr Gladstone and Mr Disraeli.

Such was the success of her 'Establishment' that Mrs Byers had to move to larger premises, first to 10 Howard Street and then c.1863 to a purpose built large double house at 74-76 Pakenham Place, Dublin Road, which provided classrooms and dormitories for the pupils as well as accommodation for teachers and a home for Margaret and her son. By 1874 the school had outgrown even these premises and so, fundraising among former pupils, their parents, and her own influential friends, Mrs Byers acquired the corner site on University Road and Lower Crescent from the Corry family and commissioned Young and MacKenzie to design a building to her own, very precise, specifications. So forward thinking was she in her design of this school building that it was only in 1972 that the school moved to its present Cranmore Park site, although it had had to expand into adjacent buildings along Lower Crescent at various times during the intervening 100 years. The building is still fulfilling its role in education as the location of the Crescent Arts Centre. For many years, before the purchase of Drumglass House in the 1920s, the top floor of the building was given over to boarding accommodation. In fact, close examination of the photographs of this accommodation in the 1908 school prospectus reveals iron bedframes that to the author's certain knowledge were still in use in the Boarding Department throughout the 1970s. The horsehair mattresses and candlewick bedspreads probably dated from 1908 as well! There was a separate infirmary/isolation ward for both staff and pupils. The school had a fully equipped domestic science classroom as well as a science lab, art studios and gymnasium as well as more traditional classrooms.

This was a huge financial undertaking but her confidence in her own abilities and those of her staff and girls paid off and in 1887, the year of the golden Jubilee, Queen Victoria commanded that the name of the school be changed to Victoria College and School. This was a great honour and was seen as official approval and respect for all that she had achieved in female education.

So why was the school so successful? One fact has to be put down to good timing. Mrs Byers was in the correct place at the correct time. She had friends who could help and support her. However this is to belittle a truly remarkable woman. Margaret Byers was passionate about women's education. She was determined that girls should have the same academic opportunities as their brothers. To this end she took on the educational establishments both at home in Ireland and also in England. Through her involvement with the Ladies' Institute in Belfast and her friendship with Isabella Tod (a leading suffragist and nineteenth century feminist) she fought for and won the right for her pupils to take their degree examinations through Royal University of Ireland. It is for this reason that the school was called a college. Until the hallowed portals of the Irish University Colleges were finally opened to both sexes in 1890, women graduates received their tuition and took their examinations through affiliated colleges, of which Victoria was one. By 1874, only 4 years after the examinations were opened up to women 13 candidates from Victoria College had won Honours certificates. Not only did Victoria College graduates top the list of women's colleges each academic year, but Victoria College Belfast came third overall after University College Dublin and University College Belfast.

While she did not fight this battle for an equal university education for women alone, as Alison Jordan says *'without the energy and enthusiasm of Mrs Byers, girls would have had to wait for even longer to realize their potential.'*

Nor was she only concerned with parity of education at University level. In 1878 she and Isabella Tod successfully lobbied in the heart of government at Westminster to have girls included in the new Intermediate Education (Ireland) Act, which provided for standardized examinations throughout all ages of school children. All the pupils at Victoria College were entered in the first examination in June 1879 – irrespective of ability.

While she was passionate about academic achievement Margaret Byers was a realist and understood that not everyone was cut out for an academic life, whether by ability or inclination. To this end she aimed to educate the whole girl and arm her with the skills to succeed in her own sphere and enrich the lives of others. Pupils received training in geometrical drawing and domestic science, and slöjd carpentry, a Swedish form of carving balsa wood. Not content with introducing the subject of Domestic Science in her own school, she lobbied the great and the good until the College of Technology in Belfast included teacher training on the subject. A life long total abstainer and Temperance Reformer, she took her concern beyond merely lecturing and was instrumental in the formation of the Victoria Homes, which operated into the 1980s and provided for poor girls from families that were unable or unwilling to care for them. As well as a good basic education the girls also received training in practical subjects which would enable them to gain and retain employment when they left the care of the homes.

Victoria College pupils were expected to fundraise for the Homes and also visit them. The pupils were also expected to visit the elderly and involve themselves in fundraising for good causes or involving themselves in social reform issues. In the early 1980s this was still the case during one's time in the Sixth Form. I have very fond memories of visiting Mrs Webb in Chadwick Street, who was a delightful lady in her late 80s. She was also a wonderful baker and, as the late, great Penny Wray and I were both starving Boarders we thoroughly enjoyed our weekly visits. She handmade our Easter eggs!

Nor were Mrs Byers's activities solely restricted to the young. She was an ardent and influential advocate for Women's Suffrage. She was an active committee member of the Ulster Branch of the National Society for Women's Suffrage.

According to Alison Jordan:

> 'she pointed out that in the Presbyterian Church of which she was a devout and devoted member, women could vote for the election of a minister and the elders. Why, she asked, could they not vote for secular office "a matter of so much less importance."'

In 1905 Margaret was awarded an honorary LLB degree by Trinity College, Dublin and in her spare time she was on the fundraising committee to build a new hospital on the Falls Road which would share at least part of its name with her own school, the Royal Victoria Hospital.

All that remains today to remind the curious about this inspirational lady is a blue plaque on the wall of Lower Crescent. And yet I would argue that she was probably one of the most influential people, of either sex, to come out of Co. Down, if not Ireland, since the Saints left Bangor in their curracles. By insisting that all teachers at Victoria College, even for the Kindergarden, had a University education she not only raised the standard of education in girls schools, but in all schools in Ireland. Even within her own lifetime she saw her innovations in education adopted not only in her own country but throughout the world as her girls ventured forth as teachers, missionaries, doctors, nurses, lawyers, and wives, taking her inspiration with them. Her legacy is seen at every graduation in Ireland, it is seen every time a girl passes a national exam. It is there every time a woman exercises her right to vote. What need has she of a statue when female education is her legacy?

ST. PATRICK AND THE EARLY SAINTS

Saints and Scholars

Partick's arrival on the banks of the Quoile near Downpatrick and his subsequent mission was to influence all of Ireland. Nowhere was that influence stronger than in Co. Down where various religious men, inspired by Patrick, set up monasteries which would produce men destined for sainthood in Ireland's golden age of Saints and Scholars.

A s someone who has lived in County Down for most of her life I am inclined to agree with a paraphrased version of Frank Pantridge's opinion of 'God's own county', but when one considers the number of saints who have made their home within the county boundaries it would be difficult to disagree. While Patrick's first, enforced, visit to Ireland was elsewhere it was to County Down that he chose to return to start his mission.

According to tradition Patrick first arrived in Ireland as a slave and worked as a swineherd for Milcho at Slemish in Co. Antrim. Following his escape and conversion he had a vision in which he:-

> *'saw a man coming, as it were from Ireland ... I imagined in that moment that I heard the voice of those very people ... and they cried out, as with one voice: "We appeal to you, holy servant boy, to come and walk among us."'*

So he decided to return to the island of his captivity, accompanied by a group of clerics. By what I choose to believe was Divine Intervention, they were blown off course and landed close to what is now called Saul in Co. Down. The author of the second life of St Patrick (who is reputed to be the nephew of the saint) tells us that

> *'He at length penetrated into a certain frith* [thought to be the Slaney]. *There, they concealed the bark, and they came a little distance into the country, that hey might rest there and lie down; and there came upon them the swineherd of a certain man of a good-natured disposition, though a heathen, whose name was Dichu, and who dwelt where now stands what is called Patrick's Barn* [Saul].'

The problem with trying to pin down details about Patrick's life is that so much was written after his death and the authors were monks who were prone to exaggeration. In fact it is not even possible to say what date he arrived with any particular certainty although the year 432 CE is generally accepted to be the start of his mission, which is the year after the arrival of St Palladius who according to the Irish Annals '... *having been ordained by Pope Celestine, is sent as first bishop to the Irish believing in Christ.'* Palladius's mission was not a great success and he was banished by the King of Leinster. Patrick was rather more successful and is now celebrated as the man who brought Christianity to pagan Ireland.

Like Amy Carmichael almost 1500 years later his mission was guided by personal conviction rather than by sanction from official church, and it led to a peculiarly Irish version of the faith, where local pagan sites of worship, such as wells, were adopted by the new faith. We are inclined to think that the conversion of Ireland was easy, however Patrick's position as a foreigner and his refusal to accept gifts from kings put him outside the normal ties of kinship and patronage. He reportedly said that on one occasion he was beaten and robbed of all that he had and held captive for 60 days.

However, succeed he undoubtedly did and within a surprisingly short period of time the island of Ireland was firmly Christian. As his mission progressed he ordained priests who in turn established monasteries to physically establish the faith in the country. Although the legend about him banishing the snakes from Ireland is false in a literal sense as there is no evidence that Ireland ever had any native snakes in the first place, the 'snakes' could refer to the followers of the original pagan faith who refused to convert. Following his death on 17th March c493 the church that he had established flourished in Ireland and produced men and women whose piety and missionary zeal leads them to be remembered a millennium and a half after their deaths. It is thought that Patrick's earthly remains were entombed at Downpatrick by St Colmcille, who had spent some time at the monastery at Movilla (Newtownards) founded by St Finnian, who had been converted by Patrick.

When one attempts to list the number of saints associated with County Down one rapidly runs out of fingers. This was particularly true during the early centuries of the church in Ireland, during the great days of the monasteries at Nendrum, Bangor and Movilla.

The earliest of these monasteries was Nendrum, on the banks of the Strangford Lough and you can still see the ruins today thanks to the excavations undertaken by the Belfast Natural History and Philosophical Society in the 1920s. Nendrum was founded c 450 by St Mochaoi, who had been converted by Patrick himself. It was an important place of worship and religious study and past pupils included St Caylan, the first Bishop of Down, and St Finnian who in turn established a monastery at Movilla, close to the present day Newtownards, and on the site of an ancient tree that had been sacred to the pagans.

Finnian's monastery was founded c540 with the help of the king of the Dál Fiatach, the ruling dynasty of what is now the eastern part of the county. Their 'captial' was at what became known as Downpatrick, which explains why Patrick was buried there. Movilla became a great centre for learning, mission and commerce and in the *Book of Armagh* Finnian is called *'A man of venerable life who reposes in many miracles in his city of Movilla'*. By the time of his death in 579 the monastery was already known outside the confines of the county thanks to one of its greatest sons, St Colmcille. It was at Movilla that Colmcille (also known as Columba) was reputed to have made his copy of the psalter, the remains of which are now housed in the Royal Irish Academy in Dublin.

Colmcille, was not the meek monk of common perception and had a stormy temperament, which led to him deciding to leave his native shores to spread his mission to the people of nearby Scotland. In 563 he set out for Scotland in a wicker currach with 12 companions. He was related to the King of Dál Riata, Conall mac Comgaill who gave him the island of Iona on which to establish his monastery. The community at Iona remains a site of spiritual retreat to this day. Some of the miracles attributed to Colmcille include turning water into wine during a communion service at Movilla and also despatching a ferocious 'water beast' to the depths of the River Ness after it had attacked one of his companions. Perhaps the first known sighting of Nessie.

While the monasteries at Nendrum and Movilla were very successful and were centres of learning as well as spiritual guidance, perhaps the most famous and also the most important of the early Christian monasteries in eastern County Down was the one established, c558, by St Comgall at Beannchor. There is a story from the twelfth century that Patrick and his companions had a vision close to the site of the monastery in which *'they beheld the valley filled with heavenly light and with a multitude of the host of heaven, they heard, as*

chanted forth from the voice of angels, the psalmody of the celestial choir.'
This led to Bangor being called the 'Valley of Angels' and the excellence of the Abbey choir was famous throughout the centuries.

Bangor Abbey was second only to Armagh as a centre of religious education and worship. Comgall established a rigid monastic rule of prayer and fasting and visitors noted that the food was very plain. Such was its importance, not only in Ireland but also throughout the British Isles that, despite there being two other Bangor monasteries in North Wales and Flinshire, our Bangor was called 'Bangor Mor' – the Great Bangor. Rev James Hamilton, himself an incumbent of Bangor Abbey 1941-79, in his *Bangor Abbey Through Fourteen Centuries* states that

> *'The studies of the monks covered a wide range of sacred and secular subjects. Biblical knowledge, with special reference to the Psalms, theology, moral and ecclesiastical law, ritual and the conduct of the services, were taught. Latin was the language of scholarship and Greek, if not formally taught, was not unknown. Greek words are to be found in the bangor Antiphonary, for example; and on the Continent it was said that if a man knew Greek, he was bound to be an Irishman.'*

However what the monastery at Bangor is best known for is training missionaries who went far beyond the confines of the British Isles and spread throughout mainland Europe. It was not for nothing that Bangor was known as the 'Light of the World'. The best known of these missionaries were Columbanus and Gall. Columbanus was born in Leinster about 543 and it is said that his mother was so distressed by his decision to follow a monastic life that she threw herself across the threshold to prevent him from leaving the house. In spite of real or perceived maternal restraint Columbanus eventually made his way to Bangor where he was a pupil, disciple and friend of Comgall. In 589 he set out with twelve companions, including Gall, travelling through Scotland

and England to Burgundy in Gaul. The Bangor monks were horrified at what they found in Gaul. The fall of the Roman Empire had led to almost constant warfare and the region was largely depopulated, with churches in ruins and *'the power of religion was regarded as almost extinct'*. According to Hamilton *'the forests around them were full of bears and wolves, and the people were all pagans.'* Undeterred the monks did what they knew best and founded monasteries at Anagray, Luxeuil and Fontaines. These were governed by rules set down by Columbanus, influenced by the severity of the regime established by Comgall at Bangor. The Rule at Luxeuil is the only monastic Rule of Irish origin which still survives and gives us an idea of what life would have been like for the monks at Bangor.

It was during this mission that the differences between the Roman Church and the Irish Church, which were there from the early days of Patrick's mission, came to the fore and resulted in great tension. Columbanus was more than able to defend the Celtic Church, but it resulted in him being expelled from the area. He was determined to go to Italy and set off up the Rhine to Switzerland. Gall fell ill at Bregenz and was left behind to be nursed at Arbon. Gall was not as forceful or driven as Columbanus and led the life of a hermit in the forests close to Lake Constance. He attracted followers, due to his gifted preaching, but limited the number to twelve, as he did not want to form a monastery. He turned down requests to become both Bishop of Constance and head of the monastery of Luxeuil, preferring a life of solitude. He is often depicted with a bear as there is a legend that he was lying in a clearing in the forest one evening when a bear came charging out of the woods. He put his hand up and told it to go away and the bear stopped and retreated back into the woods. However it reappeared shortly afterwards carrying firewood in its mouth and for the rest of its life was his constant companion. Gall died c. 648.

Columbanus and his remaining companions continued into North Italy where Columbanus founded his last monastery at Bobbio, Lombardy c.612. Although he was an old man he is supposed to have taken an active part in the physical construction of the monastery as well as its spiritual construction. As with the monasteries in France the monastery at Bobbio gained a reputation as a centre of learning and the strict observance of the Rules inherited from Comgall. The library at Bobbio was to become the home of many priceless manuscripts taken there to save them from the attentions of the Vikings in later centuries. Of these the most famous was the *Antiphonary of Bangor*, which is a seventh century manuscript that was created in Bangor. It includes the Commemoration of our Abbots which includes the lines *'Christ loved Comgall, well too did he, the Lord'*.

Worn out by his travels and old age Columbanus retreated to a cave outside Bobbio and above the River Trebbia, where he built a chapel and it was here that he died in 615. It has been calculated that between them Columbanus and his 12 companions were directly responsible for the establishment of 105 monasteries. Each of these monasteries in their turn became the source of mission. Hamilton quotes C W Previte-Orton who said that

> *'The healthiest and most zealous life of the Frankish Church was to be found in the monasteries ... founded from 585 onwards by the Irish monk, St Columbanus and his disciples ... These monks not only preserved learning and devotion, they were informed by a missionary spirit (and) their zeal was an inspiring force for present and future.'*

AMY CARMICHAEL
1867–1951
Missionary

Born in Millisle, Amy became a missionary in the
Tinnevelly district of south India where she and the
work she did for poor and exploited children is still
fondly remembered today.

If you are driving past Hamilton Road Presbyterian Church in
Bangor your eye might be caught by a small bronze statue placed
outside the Welcome Centre. Given Presbyterians' aversion to statues your interest may be piqued enough to enquire whom it rep-
resents and the answer is the subject of this essay. Other than the
fact that the World Wide Missionary Convention has been held
annually in HRPC for decades, Amy Carmichael had no known
connection with the congregation. However she was a missionary
whose influence is still felt by the community that she chose to
serve.

Amy Carmichael was born in 1867 into a prosperous Presbyterian
family from Millisle, Co. Down. Her parents, David and Catherine,
were devout members of their local congregation and ensured that
all their seven children received a firm grounding in the principles
of their religion. Eric J Sharpe in his biography of Amy in the

International Bulletin of Missionary Research, notes that the young Amy was 'impulsive, headstrong and tomboyish' – traits that were not dimmed during her short education in a Methodist boarding school in Harrogate, Yorkshire where she was remembered as having been *'a rather wild Irish girl who was often in trouble with the mistresses'* and as *'something of a rebel.'* Perhaps it was her own memories of this rebelliousness that made her so understanding of them in others, later in her life.

Amy's life would probably have continued upon traditional lines of education, marriage and motherhood, had it not been for a dramatic reversal in the family's finances. Her father and uncle owned a large flour milling business and, during the 1880s, opened new premises in Belfast. Unfortunately unwise investments and an imprudent loan to a family member, which was defaulted upon, resulted in the business going bankrupt. The family home in Millisle was sold, Amy and her younger brothers were brought home from their schools in England and the family moved to Belfast. More distress followed with the premature death of her father, David, at the age of 54 in 1885 when Amy was still in her teens.

One Sunday morning, Amy and her family were walking home from a church service when she noticed an old woman, dressed in rags and with a shawl over her head, struggling to carry her bags in the pouring rain. Other churchgoers were ignoring her, passing by on the other side of the road, but Amy and her brothers went to help her carry her burden home. This started her on an amazing course of action. It would have been both reasonable and acceptable for her to have returned home basking in the glow of having done a good deed, perhaps including the poor in general in her daily prayers more frequently or trying to raise funds for one of the many charities for the poor. Amy, however, was not an average teenage girl. In a few short months she had organized a Sunday School for the 'shawlies' in Rosemary Street Presbyterian Church

Hall. Shawlies were the poor women of the city who could not afford to buy a hat and so used to cover their heads with shawls. Not content with the Sunday School, where the women were also taught to read and write, and with visiting the poor on Saturday nights, Amy decided that she had to provide the poor with their own church, where they might feel more welcome. To that end she solicited funds to buy a tin hall, and the land on which to site it, from rich benefactors, and so started the Welcome Centre, Cambrai Street, Belfast, which still operates to this day.

Given her obvious interest in mission work among the poor at home, it is not surprising that she should have attended a 'convention of Keswick lines' in Glasgow in 1886. The Keswick mission thought that it was possible for a Christian to live a life of faith free from the stain of sin and omissions. When James Hudson Taylor (1832-1905, founder of the China Inland Mission) and Robert Wilson (1825-1905, a Cumbrian industrialist and Quaker) were the guest speakers at the Belfast convention in 1887, they were invited to dine at the Carmichael's home. Amy's life was about to change forever.

Robert Wilson was a 62 year old widower who had recently lost his only daughter. Amy was not yet 20 years old and she had recently lost her beloved father. There was an immediate, platonic, connection. The two entered into what was to become a life-long correspondence and by 1890 Amy had moved to live with Wilson and his two sons at Broughton Grange, just outside Keswick, to live as an (unofficial) adopted daughter. From around this time until well after his death Amy would sign herself as Wilson-Carmichael. However, if Wilson had thought that she would remain at home to comfort him in his old age he was mistaken.

Amy always said that she could exactly date the day she received her 'call' to go to the missions. Writing of the 13th January 1892 she said *"I cannot be mistaken, for I knew He spoke. He says 'Go', I cannot stay."* And go she did.

Sharpe says that 'for a few years Amy's life can be described only as chaotic'. She initially wanted to go to the China Inland Mission, but was turned down on the grounds of ill-health, and so set off instead to Japan in March 1893. She does not appear to have told anyone that she was arriving, but was made welcome when she appeared. However, in July 1894, she was sent to China to recuperate from constant migraines. While en-route she suddenly decided that God was calling her to travel to Sri Lanka instead. As Sharpe notes:

> *'Without officially notifying anyone at home of her intentions, still less asking for permission, she simply left for Colombo, assuming no doubt that everyone at home would immediately see things her way. That her precipitate action might be seen as irresponsibility seems hardly to have crossed her mind.'*

Her stay in Sri Lanka was short lived, however, as Robert Wilson suffered a stroke and she had to return to England in November 1894. Over the next few months Amy decided to put her missionary instincts on a more formal and professional basis. She applied to and was accepted by the Church of England Zenana Missionary Society, and arrived in India in November 1895. She never left.

In the 'faith mission' circles in which she moved, formal training was not considered to be necessary. Amy, however, was not convinced that speaking loudly and slowly in English was not the best way to win hearts and minds and so decided that learning Tamil would be a better way to further her mission. She made contact with a Church of England missionary called Thomas Walker, who was working in the Tinnevelly district of south India, who invited her to join his mission and her decision to accept his invitation changed not only her own life but that of thousands of others.

Nowadays we are often conflicted about the role of missionaries, especially in the nineteenth century when it was used as a wing of colonialism. The image of well-meaning white women in full Victorian corsetry, saving the souls of little foreigners is one which makes many feel uneasy. There is always the thought that at the heart of it is an inherent racism.

Amy was not in any way conflicted. She was a Christian. She thought that anyone who was not a Christian was wrong and called them 'heathens'. She thought that many of the practices of non-Christians were evil and inspired by Satan. And when it came to the existence of the Devadasi system, she was quite certain that it was wrong. As initially conceived this system was along the same lines as the religious communities found throughout the world, including convents and monasteries. High caste families would dedicate one of their children to the service of a temple and its god becoming a 'Devadasi' who were considered to represent the God or Goddess. However when Amy encountered it, the practice had often become a cover for religious prostitution and paedophilia.

Amy was horrified and determined to do whatever she could to 'rescue' the young girls from their fate. When she was a child herself Amy had always lamented the fact that she had brown eyes and dark hair, however these physical traits now assisted her in her mission. She adopted the local way of dressing and styling her hair. This made her appear more approachable for the young girls she wanted to save. If she had been a blue-eyed blond woman in western dress they would have been too scared to go near her.

In Tinnevelly she was confronted by the truth of the exploitation of both women and children in the name of custom and or religion. Sharpe describes her attitude best

"The white heat of her anger was reserved for the treatment meted out, in the name of religion to women and children: temple prostitution, infant and child marriage, 'merchandise in children's souls",

these outraged her and she had the ability to say so without sounding merely shrill."

She was equally contemptuous of the western missionary societies, which glossed over the realities and sent sanitised reports home. She felt that the public who supported the missions deserved to hear the truth.

In 1901 a young temple girl called Preena, ran away from the Temple and asked her for help. By 1904 she had 17 children under her care and as the years went by so more and more children were rescued or abandoned at her gate. The school for girls (boys were admitted much later) which she established at Dohnavur is still thriving today, half a century or more after her death. It has helped thousands of young girls to escape the poverty of their birth and to receive an education and equip themselves for a useful and independent life.

Nor can a modern commentator label her as racist. The community that she established was run by and for the local community. While she was still actively involved in it she was the undisputed head, however she encouraged and promoted local women within the organisation. In fact there was a famous disagreement with the entire Neill family which illustrates this point. Dr and Mrs Neill and their son, Stephen, were sent out by the Church Mission Society who were helping to provide funds for the school. Both of the parents were doctors and their medical skills were much needed in the school. The son Stephen had recently graduated from Cambridge university and was about to embark on a career in the Church of England. The family thought that they were better suited to leading the community than Amy and her band of native assistants, most particularly in the field of religious instruction and preaching. Amy chose to disagree. The parents were encouraged to move on within 6 months and did so in very bad grace, mutterings of 'Plymouth Brethren non-conformism' were aimed at Amy. Stephen

Neill, stuck it out for a few months longer but such was the degree of disagreement between him and Amy that not only did she sever her connections with the Church of England Zenana Mission, but when he became the Anglican Bishop of Tinnevell (with pastoral responsibility for the geographical area than included Dohnavur) Amy severed all connections with the Anglican Church.

Due to increasing ill-health, for the last couple of decades of her life Amy had to withdraw from the day-to-day administration of the school. She spent her time writing books and articles, many of which are still available today. As a result she became one of the best known missionaries in the world. When she died on the 18th January 1951 she was buried in the garden of the school and community she had founded. Over her grave was placed a bird-bath with one word on it. Ammai – Mummy.

Amy was an uncompromising bible Christian. She did not really see herself as belonging to any particular sect. For her belief in Christ the Redeemer was all. Your gender or race was immaterial. Your religious belief was everything. For her the basic message was that God is Love. Every child under her care was tucked into bed at night, given a kiss and told that they were loved. No child was physically punished. No child was reprimanded for youthful exuberance. The only crime that was punished was lying. During my research into her life and mission I came across a short clip of a programme made about Amy for the BBC by their Indian Correspondent, Mark Tully. Half a century after her death he was interviewing three very old ladies who had been pupils in her school during her active mission. He asked them how they remembered her. Their faces lit up with delight and they replied with two words. "Love" and "Ammai".

Sir James Martin
1893-1981
Engineer

Crossgar native James Martin was a prolific inventor and
engineer who was at the forefront of developing safe and
reliable aircraft ejector seats. In the 60 years since the first
ejection in 1946 until 2016 his company's products have
saved 7545 lives.

As a young child I was always fascinated by a gold coloured
Corgi 'James Bond' car, which along with tyre-slashers included an ejector seat. Hours were spent pressing the button which
operated the seat and then hunting for the tiny figure. As I grew
up watching various action films each time that the hero activated
their ejector seat some adult would comment that the man who
had invented the seat came from Crossgar. That man was James
Martin.

Born into a Presbyterian farming family just outside Crossgar on
11th September 1893, James Martin was the youngest of two children born to Thomas and Sarah Martin. The household also included his grandmother and his maiden aunt Georgina. Thomas
was a bit of an inventor himself and it is a matter of conjecture
that had he lived James might never have left Co. Down. However,
when James was only 2 years old his father died very suddenly and

he was left as the only boy in a family of adoring females. This was to have a profound effect on his life. As the only boy he was allowed a degree of independence and received a degree of indulgence, especially concerning his attendance at and behaviour in school, which might have been different had his father lived.

This is not to say that he was allowed to run wild. He received a thorough Bible based education both at home and in his local Sunday School at Raffrey Presbyterian Church, equipping him with a faith that never left him. In an age when science and faith are presented as opposites, it is interesting that he never doubted that both went hand in hand and to the end of his life he had a profound faith that he expounded at every opportunity. In the authorized biography, written after his death by his great-niece Sarah Sharman, it is noted that despite not being a regular church-goer:-

'Having been brought up in a strict Presbyterian household, he had been introduced at an early age to the teachings of the Bible ... and had developed his own brand of evangelical faith which, while sometimes unorthodox, he held to with a stubborn and steadfast conviction.'

Those with whom he dealt on a business level became used to his sermonizing and use of biblical quotations. His belief that his talents were God Given gave him a degree of confidence in his own abilities that made him a formidable businessman.

By the time that his formal education came to an end at the age of 14 Martin already possessed a great and self-taught knowledge about mechanics. He was determined that he was not going to be a farmer, which upset the older generation who had been hoping that he would take over the day to day running of the family farm, and was equally determined that he was not going to continue in formal education. There had been an attempt to tutor him for matriculation at the Queen's College, Belfast Engineering Department, but he deliberately sabotaged his admission interview, so it came to nothing. He was passionate about how machines worked and wanted to make his own designs. Later in his life he wrote:-

'I had always got the notion that I wanted to design things and not to be employed by anyone. It was always my policy that I must have a place of my own, to be free to work on my own inventions and develop them.'

While he did not want to enter into an apprenticeship or work for someone else he was happy to learn from others. He was passionately interested in motor cars and haunted the Belfast factories where they were made, watching each stage of production on the shop-floor and closely questioning the mechanics and engineers. It was also at this time that he first became interested in aeroplanes. Most people associate Harry Ferguson with tractors, however he was also an early designer of aeroplanes. The young Martin visited Ferguson's Belfast workshop and watched the construction of Ferguson's 'plane. Together with his friend Joe, he watched the first flight of the 'plane in 1909, later recalling:-

'I remember seeing Harry Ferguson in his aeroplane on the grounds of the Slieve Donard Hotel where he used to run it up. If my memory serves me right, it was fitted with a Clarkson propeller and the engine, I believe suffered from overheating. In order to get over this, a ring of holes was drawn round each cylinder so that a certain proportion of exhaust could escape from these holes. The net result was the oil was thrown out through these holes and they had to be tapped and fitted with short play screws.'

Ever the engineer!

It was just two years later, in 1911, that he made his first application to the Patent Office in London. This concerned an invention of a speed alarm for aeroplanes. Due to his ignorance about the correct way to fill in the paperwork he was not granted the patent, but it was just the first of many applications over the next decades.

For the next few years Martin lived at home and continued his non-conformist education in the mechanics of engines. The type of engine was immaterial to him, what he wanted to know was how it worked and how could it be improved. Such was his single-mindedness that the turmoil of the First World War and Home Rule crises barely featured on his consciousness. His mother continued to try to interest him in agriculture, but unless he was tinkering with an engine he was not interested. He began to build a small business for himself making engines for a local council and a businessman on the Isle of Man amongst others, but he was largely supported by his family.

In August 1919 he decided that the opportunities for an aspiring engineer and businessman would be better in a big city than Crossgar, a decision which saw Martin, then aged 26, arrive in London with the grand sum of £10 to his name. His sister Jane had married Edwin Burrell the previous year and set up home in Acton, so in was natural that James should take rooms close by.

His first priority was to set up a business for himself and so he managed to find a rundown garage from which he could operate. He managed to equip the workshop by touring salvage yards and other workshops in the hunt for old and unwanted machinery. He even managed to acquire a workbench by salvaging several wooden planks and transporting them back to his workshop by bus. He also began to make contacts with other mechanics and engineers in an attempt to get offered jobs. However it was very slow going and, despite being a very hard worker, eventually his money began to run out. He could not afford the rent on both his digs and his workshop so he gave up the digs and moved in with Jane and her husband Edwin. It could be argued that Edwin is an unsung hero in the story of James Martin's life. There can not be many husbands who are willing, let alone happy, to have their rather eccentric brother-in-law move in with them shortly after their marriage. Still fewer who would still give them house room when the brother-in-law thought that the kitchen was a proper place to strip down and rebuild a motorbike. However, the saintly Edwin not only put up with James and his engineering projects, but did so for almost 20 years.

Martin himself always retold a story from his early years in England, which he said shaped his entire life. Shortly after arriving in Acton he befriended a young South African evangelist, who invited him back to his lodgings for a very scant meal of reheated tea and dry bread. It turned out that he owed £25 in back rent to his landlady who had taken his good suit and a gold watch as security, so was living on bread and tea until he could redeem them. Despite the fact that he only had £30 to his name James gave him the £25. Later that night he opened his bible for his daily reading and read:- *In as much as you do it to the least of these my brethren, you do it unto Me.'* He always believed that *'It was a test but I did not fail, and God has blessed me enormously over the years.'*

As his reputation as an engineer began to grow he had to look for larger premises and so rented a barn at Friar's Place Farm, which had replaced pasture land with tennis courts rented out to local clubs, and came to an arrangement to convert the horse drawn grass cutters into motorized ones. It was also at this time that he met his lifelong assistant, Eric Stevens, while on a visit to Napier's factory. Together they bought army surplus lorries in Slough, which they would overhaul or modify before selling them on at a small profit. In his youth Martin had become quite an accomplished black-smith and so was able to save money by doing his own ironwork.

In November 1923 he applied for his first English based patent. It was a design for a light body frame for vehicles that could be used as either an open trailer or an enclosed lorry. This time he employed a Patent Agent, George Raynor, to do the paperwork and it was accepted in 1925. Unfortunately, as was the case for a number of years, he lacked the financial backing to start manufacturing it himself.

With Brooklands motor racing circuit close at hand, it was not surprising that James would become interested in the sport. He bought and modified a second hand yellow French Salmson car. Martin and Stevens took part in a number of races, however their sporting career came to a dramatic end during the 1928 Ulster Tourist Trophy race when the brakes failed and car and passengers ended up in a butcher's shop in Comber. While he gave up racing cars he continued to drive at speed for the rest of his life, much to the consternation of the less courageous of his passengers. It might be argued that he used his driving as part of his evangelizing – if you didn't believe in the power of prayer before you sat in the passenger seat you certainly did by the time you got out of the car!

Around this time Martin joined the London Aero Club and forged two friendships that changed his life. The first was with Valentine Baker, the handsome and famous First World War pilot, and the second was with Amy Johnston. His friendship with both was to last for the rest of their lives.

With these new connections with aviation it was natural that the focus would move in that direction as well and on 3rd August 1929 Martin's Aircraft Works was established in Denham, Buckinghamshire, in an old linoleum factory purchased by long suffering brother-in-law, Edwin Burrell and rented to James. The Martin Baker company is still on the same site today. James, Eric and two further employees, Jim Chadwin and Philip 'Jimboy' Clampitt, moved everything from the Acton workshop on the back of a horse and cart. It was shortly after this move that he decided to design his first aeroplane. Consulting closely with Valentine Baker and Amy Johnston over frequent late dinners, it was decided that Amy should be the test pilot for the new 'plane and she often visited the Denham factory to see how it was progressing. Unfortunately the 'plane never materialized as Martin ran out of money, however it was not his last collaboration with Amy Johnston.

Martin had suggested to Amy that she should fly solo to Australia, to make her name and fortune. She was very enthusiastic about the project and managed to get financial backing to proceed. When she flew to Croydon on 4 May 1930 Martin was there to do a final check on the 'plane before her departure on the 5th. She was going to carry a spare propeller strapped to the fuselage of the plane and he was worried that it might be sabotaged, stolen or damaged during the night, so he took it home with him and stored it in Edwin's front hall. Sarah Sharman comments that *History does not relate what Edwin had to say about this overnight visitor.*

On the 5th May Amy's departure was held up by several minor problems, including a broken watch, all of which James was able to rectify and with him standing on the runway acting as a marker for her take-off, she rose into the air and into history. Such was their friendship that she had asked him to act as her agent and sell her story to Fleet Street newspapers.

James's perennial problem was lack of money. He was now in his 40s and while his ideas were plentiful his bank balance was arid. While driven and hard working without the funds to put his ideas into production he could not proceed. However his friendship with Valentine Baker was to prove very profitable. Baker made a living by acting as a flying instructor at Heston Flying Club. One of his pupils was Francis Francis, who fortunately possessed more imagination than his parents. Francis was married to an American actress called Sonny Jarman and was the possessor of a large fortune. Baker introduced Francis to James and the three men became firm friends. Sarah Sharman says that *their friendship has been described as magic.* Francis was eager to provide the funds for a new aeroplane designed for civilian use, and as the project progressed he decided that the *ad hoc* arrangement should be put on a more formal footing. He suggested that Martin and Baker should form a company that he would fund. For James, then aged 41,

> *'with a lifetime of design work behind him but little to show for it, the opportunity of having a company with the financial resources to enable him to build the superlative aircraft he believed he was capable of was the answer to his prayers.'*

Sharman

The Martin-Baker Aircraft Company was formed in 1934 and their first aircraft project was the MB1 a two-seat light touring aircraft but, with the storm clouds of war gathering, the company's focus moved from civillian aircraft to those needed by the military. This resulted in the Martin-Baker MB2, a private venture project designed to meet Air Ministry Specification F.5/34 for a fighter for service in the tropics. The MB2 was tested but neither it nor other designs to F.5/34 were adopted.

Since even before the company's inception in 1934 James Martin had recognised the difficulty of making an emergency escape from the new breed of high speed aircraft and had begun initial investigations into assisted escape systems. This work led him to focus in on power assisted ejector seats which would lift the pilot out of the cockpit and clear of the aircraft, a similar conclusion reached by Swedish and German research teams some years later.

However, at this time the company was not only developing complete aircraft, it was also designing and manufacturing aircraft components, including ammunition belt feeds and armoured seats for Supermarine Spitfires, (which it did throughout the Second World War). This meant that work on ejection seats was somewhat put on the back-burner where it may have remained were it not for a fatal accident during the testing of the company's third prototype, the MB3 which resulted in the death of Martin's friend and business partner, Valentine Baker.

This accident in 1942 affected Martin so much that pilot safety became his primary focus and led to the later reorganisation of the company to focus primarily on ejection seats. Thus when in 1944, the Ministry of Aircraft Production sought a company to develop methods for fighter pilots to escape their aircraft, the Martin Baker Company was the obvious choice.

The first 'live' ejection with a man in the seat occurred in 1946 when Bernard Lynch ejected from a Gloster Meteor travelling at 320 miles per hour over Chalgrove Airfield in Oxfordshire.

The system based on James Martins ideas was so successful that in the 70 years up to 2016 over 7500 pilots had ejected safely from their stricken aircraft.

At last financially secure James bought himself a home and moved out of Edwin and Jane's house. Then he found himself a wife, Muriel, who was prepared to put up with his work obsession and eccentricity. One of his passions was guns and he owned several, including a Sten gun. Ever curious as to how machines worked and how they could be improved he once demonstrated an old Sten gun for his children on the front lawn. They were more impressed by the fact that their mother did not come out to see what they were up to than by the demonstration. He had twin sons and two daughters on whom he doted.

As the company went from strength to strength and began to work closely with the RAF, especially during the Second World War, Martin became more and more frustrated by officialdom. He was still raging against the inability of governments of both parties to listen to businessmen rather than academics when it came to promoting home-grown, independent companies. The high rates of taxation was another bugbear as he felt that it stunted growth at both a person and business level.

Shortly before his death at the age of 87 on 5th January 1981 he wrote the following:

> *(I have) always been interested in design work, even as a child. I have taken out some 150 patents all over the world for various things. I am also capable of doing any kind of machine work in any works – milling, grinding, drilling, tool making and so on – anything to do with mechanical engineering. ... It has never been my ambition to acquire large sums of money. I always try to give the highest possible standard of design married to the best workmanship. ... There is far too much emphasis put on college degrees. ... Here at these Works there are only a couple of people with any degrees, but the rest have got something which cannot be got at Universities – they have know-how which has been developed over a period of years. ...I suppose it is fair to say that a certain amount of people are born into the world that can create something out of nothing – new ideas, new schemes and so on. Why have those people got that particular ability? There is only one answer – the Creator. The Creator made everything out of nothing.*

While doing the research for this essay I often wondered how James Martin would fair in today's society. The hyperactive, disruptive schoolboy would no doubt be labelled with some disorder. His lack of academic qualifications would prevent him from getting employment in his chosen profession and his inability to fill in official paperwork would prevent him from gaining either recognition for his designs or financial backing from banks. His driven, single-minded approach to work would be seen as a manifestation of Obsessive Compulsive Disorder. And, sadly, his unflinching and unapologetic Bible based faith would be derided in the scientific community. All of which makes us the poorer.

MAJOR-GENERAL
ROBERT ROSS
1766-1814

Soldier

Fought with distinction under the Duke of Wellington in
various European campaigns before being dispatched to the
USA during the Anglo-American war of 1812-14.
He led a successful attack on Washington DC
occupying the city and torching both the Capitol
building and the White House.

On the 5th September 2014 the Newry and Mourne District
Council Facebook page proudly posted that:-

> *'70 school children from Rostrevor took part in a unique "living
> flag" event in Rostrevor, County Down as part the upcoming Star
> Spangled Rostrevor Festival. School children from St Bronagh's,
> Kilbroney Integrated and Killowen Primary Schools hoisted a giant
> 42 ft X 30 ft replica of the original Star Bangled Banner Flag which
> flew over Fort Mc Henry at the end of the 1812-14 War, coinciding
> with the writing of the American National Anthem by Francis Scott
> Key in September 1814.'*

Now what, one might ask had that to do with either the subject
of this essay, or indeed with Rostrevor? The answer is quite simple. Robert Ross, from Rostrevor, was the man who set fire to the
White House and inspired the lyrics to the American National
Anthem, the Star Spangled Banner.

Robert Ross came from the gentry. His father, Major David Ross, had served in the Seven Year War (1756-1763) and his mother was the half-sister of the Earl of Charlemont.

Ross was educated at Trinity College, Dublin, where he became Treasurer of the College Historical Society, before graduating with a BA 1789. He married Elizabeth Glasscock while still at University and their son, also called Robert, was born in 1788. It was a very happy marriage and Ly, as he called her, was devoted to her husband and even followed him on his military adventures. They had another son, David, and a daughter, Elizabeth, before Robert's untimely death.

Our Robert was a contemporary of both Rollo Gillespie and Arthur Wellesley, Duke of Wellington and like them joined the army for something to do and as a chance of making their fortune or finding some adventure. This was a usual step for many a young man of a vaguely aristocratic background. The army offered a chance for adventure, a good social life (think of the characters in Jane Austen's novels) and also the chance of enrichment as the 'spoils of war' – i.e. anything that was able to be looted – was considered to be fair game to be divided out amongst the officers and men.

And so it was that Ross enlisted in the 25th Foot as an Ensign on 1st August 1789. Over the next decade or so he saw active service with several regiments and his skill as both a soldier and an officer saw him advance up the ranks. In 1799 he joined the 20th Foot as a Major and by September 1801 had been given command of the regiment following the successful attack on French held Alexandria, Egypt in January of the same year.

By 1808 when he and the 20th were sent to the Iberian Peninsula he was a Lieutenant Colonel and distinguished himself in the otherwise disastrous retreat from La Corunna in 1809. The 20th were then sent to Walcheren in the Netherlands, which was a disaster not just militarily but medically as 'Walcheren Fever' literally decimated the British Forces. 4,000 out of 40,000 men died from fever compared to 100 killed in action. Ross and his regiment were sent back to Ireland to recuperate. However Ross did not remain long in his native land as he was made an aide-de-camp to King George III on 25th July 1810. This was something of a poisoned chalice as it was in December of this year that George once more succumbed to the illness that manifested itself in a descent into madness and Ross must have witnessed this descent at first hand.

On 28th October 1812 Ross and the 20th once more landed on the Iberian Peninsula, this time under the command of his fellow Irishman, Arthur Wellesley, who was sufficiently impressed with his ability to give him command of the fusilier brigade and promoted him to Major-General on 4th June 1813. Ross had a 'good war' and was awarded a medal for his leadership at the battle of Vitoria, however at the battle of Orthez in February 1814 he received a near fatal wound to his neck. The ever-devoted Elizabeth rode on horseback through the snow of the Pyrenees to tend to her wounded hero.

As an officer Ross was known to be a great stickler for training and discipline, but his men were devoted to him and he was known to entertain them by playing on his violin, or fiddle. They knew him to be a courageous, if slightly reckless, soldier and commanding officer who led from the front. In fact, he had several horses killed under him in the heat of battle. Later an American prisoner of Ross would say that *he was the perfect model of the Irish gentleman, of easy and beautiful manners, humane and brave ... and his prisoners had no reason to regret falling into his hands.* Given that he had been wounded in action General and Mrs Ross could be forgiven for thinking that they could return to their home on the shore of Carlingford Lough for some rest and recuperation. However, events across the Atlantic were to change their plans when America declared war on Britain in one of the most unnecessary conflicts of all times.

Lord Castlereagh had removed one of the main causes of the conflict 6 days before the American Declaration of War by lifting the trade restrictions that had been aimed more at revolutionary French ships than American (although in effect this had amounted to the same thing) but there were other causes: The Americans attacking the territory to the north that later became Canada; the allegation that British forces in the north were recruiting Native Americans to attack the American settlements; the Royal Navy's habit of boarding American ships and press-ganging anyone with a 'British' accent into the Royal Navy; and finally, but by no means least, Vice Admiral Sir Alexander Cochrane's habit of bombarding the eastern seaboard towns from his ship HMS Tonnant (which had been seized at the battle of the Nile).

Everything was shaping up towards an outbreak of hostilities between the two nations and, despite the Duke of Wellington's reservations, Ross and his battle hardened men were despatched to the other side of the Atlantic. Among his men were two key aides who had served with him in Spain and France. Harry Smith, who had married a Spanish lady, and fellow Irishman George de Lacy Evans a young cavalry officer who won a medal for leading his dragoons in repeated charges at the battle of Vitoria.

When Cochrane received a letter from General George Prevost telling of outrages committed by Americans in a raid on British North American territories, he ordered *'retributory justice into the country of our enemy … to destroy and lay waste such towns and districts upon the coast as you find assailable.'* Cochrane's willingness to take this step may have been influenced by the fact that his brother had been killed, 33 years earlier, at Yorktown in one of the last major encounters of the War of Independence.

The attack was to be a combined effort between the army and the navy with Ross in command of the army and Rear Admiral George Cockburn in charge of the naval personnel. This was not a small force. Ross had under his command around 4,000+ men, most of whom had seen action against the French in Europe. He organised them into three brigades of between 1,100 and 1,500 each and had four regiments to call upon, amongst whom was the 4th King's own which had fought for King Billy at the battle of the Boyne and the 44th under the command of fellow Ulsterman Colonel Arthur Brooke. However, he had no cavalry and had only three artillery pieces, as he was not sure that he would be able to find any horses and so had to rely upon sailors to drag the guns. To confuse the enemy as to their real target they advanced by boat up both the Patuxent and Potomac rivers as far as they could before landing the troops and guns. This was not an army of occupation; instead it was a sophisticated and well-armed raiding party.

There was no expectation that they would reach their primary goal of attacking Washington. Although the bulk of the American 'army' was occupied elsewhere, namely mounting the raids Prevost had complained about, there was still a militia and the Americans were not going to allow them to advance unimpeded.

However, the local slave population supported the British. Britain had abolished the slave trade in 1807 and while there were around 2,000 slaves in what became Canada, they had been brought by people fleeing the War of Independence. In fact following a series of court cases in 'Canada' in the 1790s it had been ruled that *the slave could not be compelled to served longer than he would and … might leave his master at will.'* Cockburn and Ross were under instructions not to free any slaves they encountered, in case this led to a slave revolt along the lines of Haiti, but if slaves wanted to leave their masters and join the British forces then that was allowed. Both men were very impressed by the calibre of the slaves who flocked with their families to the British side and Cockburn wrote that they *'are really very fine fellows'*.

Undoubtedly the British were assisted by the incompetence of the American administration and leadership. President James Madison was one of the country's founding fathers and was once described as looking like a schoolmaster dressed for a funeral. A great politician, he was however no George Washington. This was made worse by his choice of John Armstrong as War Secretary and Brigadier General William Winder as military commander. Armstrong thought that if Ross did attack Washington *'it will necessarily be a mere Cossack Hurrah, a rapid march and hasty retreat'*, but did suggest a sensible course of action. He advised that in the event of an attack the Americans should retreat to the Capitol building and defend it with the 5,000 militia men available and a battery of guns. Instead Winder did the exact opposite and moved to engage with the British forces at Bladensburg, 5 miles north-east of Washington.

When the good citizens of Washington learnt of the approach of the Red Coats they threw as much as they could carry on to carts and fled the city. Madison advised his wife, Dolley, to do the same but she refused. To give him credit, Madison stayed with his militiamen on the field of battle, the only President other than Lincoln to do so. However it was all in vain. The untrained reservists were no match for the battle-hardened British and by teatime it was all over and there was nothing to stop the march on Washington.

With the support of Cockburn, the triumphant Ross set fire to both houses of Congress in the Capitol building that Armstrong had suggested defending. They then advanced on the recently completed White House. Mrs Madison fled, pausing only to rescue a portrait of George Washington and her red curtains. In fact the dining table was already laid and the dinner was still warm in the kitchens. The British soldiers helped themselves to the meal and then, surrounding the building they smashed the windows and hurled in torches. Within minutes the whole building was ablaze.

Other than setting fire to the main buildings in the city, the British behaved very well to those citizens who had remained and even paid for supplies. Ross in a letter dated 1st September said that

'I trust all our differences with the Yankees will shortly be settled. That wish is, I believe, very prevalent with them. They feel strongly the disgrace of having had their capital taken by a handful of men and blame very generally a government which went to war without the means or the abilities to carry it on ... The injury sustained by city of Washington in the destruction of its public buildings has been immense and must disgust the country with a government that has left the capital unprotected.'

Flushed with their success at the capital, Ross and Cochburn turned their attention to nearby Baltimore, a mere 30 miles north-east of Washington. Baltimore was then one of America's richest cities. They set sail once more and were landed around 16 miles away from the city while the Royal Navy bombarded Fort McHenry, which guarded the city's harbour, for 25 hours. This time the militiamen who were defending the city were rather better organised and the attack was repelled. It was in the morning after the bombardment that the young Francis Scot Key wrote a poem *Defence of Fort M'Henry* whose words would in time become the lyrics of the American National Anthem, *The Star Spangled Banner.*

The opening line of the poem is *'O say can you see, by the dawn's early light'*, but Ross never saw that dawn's early light. On 12th September, shortly after landing at North Point with Cockburn and their troops he was shot by a sniper. The musket ball ripped through his arm, into his chest. He died while being transported back to the ships. One of his aides recorded that his last words were 'O! My beloved wife and family ...' His body was stored in a barrel of Jamaican run and shipped to Halifax in Nova Scotia, where he was buried on 24 September 1814.

GEORGE BEST

1946-2005

Footballer

Widely regarded as one of the greatest players the game of
football has ever produced he was one of the first to break
out of the 'Roy of the Rovers' mold to become a playboy
superstar with tragic results.

Maradona Good. Pele Better. George Best.

One of the pleasures of writing this book is the opportunity it
gave me to watch old footage of George Best playing football
in his prime. I am not a great football fan, in fact I have only ever
watched two live matches and the highlight of the experience was
being body frisked by a young Norwegian security guard. However,
even I can see that he was in a class of his own. Add to that the fact
that he was playing with a leather ball and heavy leather football
boots with steel toecaps and his talent surpasses that of any other
player. Which makes his final years all the more tragic.

Best seemed to have everything. He was born into a loving, working class home in east Belfast, just off the Cregagh Road. His parents both worked and he and his sisters spent a lot of their time
with his grandparents, running in and out of the houses of their

extended family and friends. Belfast was just recovering from six years of war with rationing still in place and no one had very much money, but it didn't really matter, as it was the same for everyone. His father, Dickie, was a talented footballer but it was his mother Ann who had the real sporting talent in the family and she played hockey for many years, even after her children were born. As Best said himself he was obsessed with kicking a ball. *'Literally as soon as I could walk, I had a ball at my feet. ... It didn't really matter what sort of ball it was – plastic, a tennis ball, anything I could kick around. Sometimes, I would even take a ball to bed with me.'* He spent hours kicking the ball against a wall, testing himself, using alternate feet, until he was dragged indoors to bed.

When he was 11 he sat the eleven-plus exam and was the only child in his year at Nettlefield Primary School to pass. This meant that he was awarded a place in a local grammar school, Grosvenor High, but it also meant that he might have to leave association football behind as, in common with most grammar schools, Grosvenor only played rugby football. The move also meant leaving his friends behind. He didn't settle at the school and didn't really take to rugby despite describing himself as 'a pretty decent fly half' and before long had started to play truant. Given how he was to react throughout his life when confronted with a situation he didn't like it is telling that in his autobiography he confides that

> *'Truancy was just another way of running away from problems and I always did it on my own. I have always been like that and in later years, when fame became too much, I would go to Manchester Airport and get the first plane out to wherever it was going. It's an instinctive thing, kidding yourself that when you get back, the problem will have gone,'*

His parents eventually discovered his truancy and he was allowed to leave and join his friends at Lisnasharragh Secondary Modern. Saturday mornings were spent playing for the Cregagh Boy's Club team run by the Glentoran reserve team coach, Bud McFarlane who Best always credited for turning him into a footballer, frequently mentioning him in the same breath as Sir Matt Busby. Many older footballers kept telling the teenage Best that he was too small and skinny to be a professional player. McFarlane didn't agree, according to Best: *'he was the first one to really encourage me and tell me I could make it as a professional. ... Like Sir Matt he believed that if you were good enough you were both big enough and old enough.'*

However, not everything went Best's way. Aged 14 George was delighted to be picked for the Northern Ireland schoolboy squad, but when an international match was proposed he discovered that they could only afford to take a squad of 15 players and he was No. 16 so was left behind. Fortunately he had ample opportunity to pull on the green and white shirt of Northern Ireland before the end of his playing career, scoring 9 goals in 37 caps.

When Best was 15 years old McFarlane got in touch with Bob Bishop, the Manchester United scout in Northern Ireland who ran the Boyland Youth Club, and arranged a match to showcase his young star's talents. Best didn't realise at the time, but all the other players on both teams were at least 2 years older and several inches taller so that Bishop could see if he would be able to hold his own on a professional team. George scored 2 goals, securing his team's 4-2 victory and in July 1961 Bishop made a call to Matt Busby and said *"Boss, I think I've found you a genius."*

Much later, as George's career began to implode and his life went into free fall, everyone began to speculate as to where it all went wrong and many people pointed the finger at the way in which Manchester United handled their young star. However, while such an accusation is a bit unfair, the club's management should hang their heads in shame is how they arranged his initial journey over. He and Eric McMordie, neither of them old enough to drink let alone vote, were told to get the ferry over to Liverpool and then make their way to Manchester and find their way to the club. Neither of these boys had been out of Belfast by themselves any further than a train ride to Bangor, let alone travelling half way across the country.

When they eventually managed to get to Manchester they couldn't even find the ground and asked a taxi man to take them to Old Trafford. He did – the cricket ground. When they eventually found the right ground they were both overwhelmed, meeting Matt Busby, the first team players and the youth players, all of who seemed like giants to the young skinny Best. That night they locked themselves into their room in their digs and resolved to go back home. Fortunately, they were soon sent back and the rest is history.

 Best made his first team debut on 14th September 1963 at the age of 17 and was catapulted to stardom on 9th March 1966 when he scored two goals in the European Cup quarterfinal match again Benfica. I am not knowledgeable enough about football to be able to take you through each and every game he played, and in any case there are still the videos on the Internet to remind everyone of his genius on the football pitch.

Duncan Hamilton in his approved biography *Immortal* disputes the use of the word 'genius' to describe George Best at his best as the word *'has been devalued through repetition, undeservedly anointing players who alongside him seemed averagely modest.'* He continues *'He was much more than that. For five years, from the beginning of 1966 to the end of 1970, he was comprehensively better than the rest – the most accomplished player on God's earth.'* To illustrate his point, Hamilton recounts the story of how, having invited friends to watch him play one Saturday, George accepted a throw from the goalkeeper and took it to the touchline below his friends' seats in the stands. He then stood with his foot on the ball, waving to his friends as he waited for the opposition players to tackle him. Three of them converged on him. Hamilton continues *'What followed was cleverer than a conjuring trick. He smartly struck three consecutive wall passes off their legs, lifted the ball over them and ran around to regain it. He then turned, the ball still under his control, and gave his friends a bow.'*

George was one of the first homegrown superstars and no one, not his family, not his manager, not his friends, really knew how to cope with the chaos that followed him wherever he went. A rather snobby obituary printed after his death in *The Economist* says:-

'Mr Best was not simply a maker and taker of goals. He was a good looker. His fans, many of them the young women who idolised pop music stars, were happy to pay money to watch him, whether or not they understood the offside rule. In the pre-Best days no one cared about the colour of a player's eyes. Best's fans knew they were blue, just as they knew the name of the hairdresser who kept his Beatle-style hair in trim.'

Young girls broke into his landlady's house; they mobbed his car and stole his hubcaps as trophies. He opened a couple of boutiques which were mobbed if the rumour went out that he was there. He earned more money from personal appearances and endorsements than from playing football, but he couldn't enjoy a quiet night out with friends without being mobbed. He built a modern new house in Bramhall, Cheshire that he had helped to design himself with every modern gadget money could buy. However coach-loads of fans would arrive, some even picnicking on his lawn, and peer in through the windows and the planes flying overhead interfered with the remote controls for all his gadgets. He was trapped. *'When I think about it now, that house seemed to symbolise my life at the time. Chaotic, unpredictable, with nothing working as it was meant to.'*

Nowadays the club or his management team would protect him, but in the 60s no one knew what to do. The only stars bigger than George were the Beatles and even they found the pressure too much to take and retreated to India to find refuge. As he explains in his autobiography *Blessed* '

> *I was only 22 and the novelty had already long worn off. I would simply fail to turn up for events and go off on a bender instead. In the past I'd always run away in times of crises but now I turned to booze, which was much the same thing. I didn't run away physically, but mentally I escaped in the bottom of a glass.'*

He began to miss training and, on one memorable occasion, went missing for a weekend only to turn up hiding in the flat of actress Sinéad Cusack. It was only a matter of time before the club had enough of him. His last competitive game for United was on 1st January 1974. Without him they were relegated to the second division.

Over the next decade or so he continued to play football, signing with ever more average clubs and always leaving under a cloud. It was while he was playing for the Los Angeles Aztecs that he met his first wife Angie who was working as a model. They were married in Las Vegas and everything seemed to be fine. It looked as if George had finally settled down at last. Their son, Calum, was born 6th February 1981, but George's alcoholism had returned and he would disappear for days at a time on drinking binges. It is heart-breaking to read his account of Calum's birth and the first months of his life.

> *'Having Calum proved one thing – alcohol had become the most important thing in my life. More important than my wife and even more important than my new-born son. I felt guilty that I couldn't stop drinking even for him and probably drank even more because of my guilt, which is just about the worst vicious circle you could get.'*

Angie recounts the story of how she was driving down the highway near their home one day when she saw what she thought was a tramp, weaving in and out of the traffic. As she drew closer she realised it was George. She drove on past him and filed for divorce the next day. She has always maintained that she loved him, but she had a young son to care for and couldn't help a man who didn't want to be helped.

Time and time again his friends and family tried to help him to find help. The problem is that the person has to want to be helped. Along with all the clips of George at his absolute best there are also ones of him at his absolute worst, on TV chat shows, slurring his words and almost incoherent. And then there were the court cases and the prison sentences, he spent Christmas of 1984 in Ford Open Prison. And yet, and yet, there was something about him that meant that people wanted to give him another chance. When he was sober he was charming and witty. At a time when sports-men were not renowned for their intellect he was oh so funny, making light of his own misfortunes. Unlike many addicts, he did not try to blame anyone else for his problems.

In 1995 he married Alex, an air hostess, and together they tried to battle his demons. He was diagnosed with severe liver damage in March 2000 and received a liver transplant in August 2002. Alex and George moved to Ballyhalbert in an attempt to keep him away from temptation and to be closer to his own family. But even the fresh start in both location and with a new liver was not enough to keep him away from alcohol. In October 2005 he was admit-ted to intensive care at a hospital in London suffering from a kid-ney infection. On 20th November at his own request a photo was published in a newspaper showing him, bright yellow and skeletal along with a personal message about the danger of alcohol and the plea *'Don't die like me'*.

George Best died of multiple organ failure on 25th November 2005. He was 59. His body was flown home to his father's house on the Cregagh Estate, the same house he had left as a young boy in 1961. Belfast's golden boy had come home at last. Thousands of people, from both sides of the community lined the streets as his funeral cortege made its way to Parliament Buildings at Stormont for a funeral service attended by the great and the good, and by his grieving family.

'They'll forget all the rubbish when I'm gone and they'll remember the football. If only one person thinks I'm the best player in the world, that's good enough for me.'

George Best, the best soccer player in the world.

LORD CASTLEREAGH, 2ND MARQUESS OF LONDONDERRY
1769-1822

Statesman

The foremost world statesman of his day, he played a key part in the peace negotiations at the end of the Napoleonic Wars which left a legacy of relative peace in Europe for almost a century.

I have long had a secret (admiration is too strong a word) regard for a man who was almost universally both respected and loathed. I first heard about him from my father who noted that he shared his birthday and that he had died on my birthday. However the fact that he had been born just a few miles away in Mountstewart was also a hook to capture my interest. All I learnt about him and his role in two of the main events of the early nineteenth century, the Act of Union and Congress of Vienna, and the fact that the seats used at the latter are on view in Mountstewart, only served to heighten my interest. Then John Bew published a biography of him that went straight to the top of my Christmas wish list. That man was Robert Stewart, Lord Castlereagh.

Even in the late Georgian and Regency world in which he moved his list of political achievement and appointments were impressive. He was at various times Chief Secretary for Ireland, President of the Board of Control, Secretary of State for War and the Colonies, Leader of the House of Commons during Lord Liverpool's government 1812-1822 and concurrently the Foreign Secretary. He was not a man who either sought or found friends easily, but those who were his friend were devoted to him. He was the man who was in charge during the Peterloo Massacre; the man who took personal charge of the suppression of the 1798 United Irishmen rebellion; the man who bribed the turkeys in the Irish House of Commons to vote for Christmas in the form of the Act of Union in 1801. Percy B Shelley included the famous lines *'I met Murder on the way, he had a mask like Castlereagh'* in his *The Masque of Anarchy* and Lord Byron urged passers-by to 'piss' on his grave. Crowds lined the streets of London just so that they could hiss at his funeral cortege. So what is there to admire or respect about him?

Robert was born into a family that had recently married into the aristocracy. The Stewarts were originally from Scotland and had arrived in Ireland during the Plantation of Ireland. They had settled in Donegal, but by the time of Robert's birth had managed to acquire estates and land in Co. Down, specifically in Newtownards and had built their home at Mountstewart on the eastern shore of Strangford Lough. He was born in Dublin six weeks after Arthur Wellesley and the two were life long friends and at times political allies. Coincidentally a few weeks after Robert's birth a boy was born in Corsica to a Lady Bonaparte, who she named Napoleon. Robert's father (also called Robert) was a member of the Irish House of Commons, which explains why he was born in Dublin, and was a supporter of the Irish Patriot Party, led by Henry Grattan. His mother, who was related to the Dukes of Grafton, died when he was a year old and his stepmother's family members were political allies of both William Pitt the elder and younger and his step-grandfather was Lord Camden, a leading civil rights politician. It is safe to say that this was a very political family in which to be born. It was also a well-connected family and Robert continued this trend when he married Emily Hobart in 1794. Emily's mother, Caroline, was the sister of Thomas Connolly the richest man in Ireland. Thomas's wife, Louisa Lennox, was one of a group of aristocratic sisters who were direct descendants of Charles II. Louisa's sister, Emily Fitzgerald, was the Duchess of Leinster and another sister, Caroline, was the wife of Henry Fox and mother of Charles James Fox, the great Whig politician.

Unusually for someone from such a family the young Robert was sent to the Royal School at Armagh for his secondary education before heading to St John's College, Cambridge. For someone who rose to such heights within the political life of the nation it is perhaps comforting to note that he left without finishing his degree. As Ferdinand Mount so elegantly phrases it in an article in TLS *'Castlereagh's education petered out after a year at Cambridge, where he picked up nothing much except the clap.'*

According to John Bew *'The definitive moments in Castlereagh's political awakening were his visits to the Continent in 1791 and 1792, when in his early twenties.'* His grandfather had urged him to travel, telling him *'You may study books at Cambridge, but you must come into the great world to study men,'* However, the horror that he observed in France in the years when the revolution descended into the Terror was to impact his entire life. Bew notes *'As he watched the French Revolution unfold at close quarters – and studied its impact beyond France – he thought deeply about the political situation in Europe and Ireland, reaching convictions in his early life that would shape his career over the next thirty years.'*

The Stewarts were Presbyterians, or rather had recently been Presbyterians and most of their friends in Co. Down were members of the church. These included some of the leading radical Presbyterian ministers such as Rev. James Porter, who mocked them saying *'what a fine thing to see in one day, Mr changed into Lord, Mrs into My Lady; then comes the coronet painted on the coach, on the harness, on the dishes and plates, and the piss-pots'.* It was this personal connection with some of the leading men and women in the 1798 rebellion that shaped and drove Castlereagh both in the immediate aftermath of the rebellion and throughout the rest of his life. It left him with a fear of mass revolt and also with a sense of personal betrayal, however he also tried to soften the revenge that the more extreme elements within the administration were demanding. He said that he refused 'to shut the door of mercy' and so a blind eye was turned when there were burials in the dead of night or when farmers' sons slipped back into the family homestead. However, let us not kid ourselves that the retribution was not vicious and bloody. And it struck into Castlereagh's own immediate family circle. His wife Emily was a cousin by marriage of Lord Edward Fitzgerald who died of his wounds in prison and when the Rev Porter was hanged in his clerical robes it was not just a rebel strangling at the end of a rope, it was someone with whom Castlereagh had taken tea and admired.

One of the main reasons why the retribution had been so vicious was that the administration in both London and Dublin were terrified at what was happening in France. The grand ideals of Liberty, Equality and Brotherhood lay weeping at the feet of the guillotines and they were determined that it was not going to spread. The French had sent an invasion fleet, albeit a very small one, to Ireland with Wolfe Tone and the fact that the prosperous Presbyterian north had risen, when everyone thought that they would not, meant that some, including Castlereagh, determined that Ireland's Anglo-Irish aristocrats could not be trusted to govern themselves. Thus it was that the Prime Minister, William Pitt the Younger, decided that an Act of Union was the only solution.

Again Castlereagh was one of the prime movers. As a member of the Irish Privy Council he set about convincing the members of the Irish House of Commons to vote themselves out of existence.

For the most part this was achieved by bribery on a truly epic scale, with government pensions, peerages and other enticements dangled in front of their eyes. However, and this is often over-looked in many older histories that you might read, the political union that Castlereagh was trying to achieve was one which would have also included Catholic Emancipation. Given his own family's non-conformist background he was convinced that the only way to achieve lasting peace in Ireland was if all sections of society were included equally (as much as that was possible when the vote was limited to the upper echelons of society) and all equally invested in its success. In this he thought that he had the backing of the politi-cal elite in London. He was mistaken. The blame for the failure to include Catholic Emancipation in the Act of Union is often laid at the door of (mad) George III, but as the events later in the nine-teenth century were to show, it would have been very difficult to get the House of Commons at Westminster to vote it through even with the King's blessing. In the event the Act of Union was pushed through both the British and Irish Houses of Commons with very little opposition. It is worth noting here that the terms of the act were very more favourable than those of the Act of Union with Scotland a century earlier, and the Irish, or at least one section of the Irish, were very well represented in both chambers. Years later Castlereagh told the House of Commons, 'With respect to Ireland, I know I shall never be forgiven.'

When the new, united, House of Commons sat for the first time in 1801, Castlereagh was there as the MP for Down. Pitt had resigned as Prime Minister over the failure to include Catholic Emancipation in the Act of Union and the new Prime Minister, Henry Addington, appointed Castlereagh President of the Board of Control, a position he held for 4 years. In 1807, shortly af-ter the return of Pitt as PM, he was promoted again to become the Secretary of State for War and the Colonies. Pitt's health was declining and Castlereagh, as one of only two cabinet members who had a seat in the Commons, took over more and more of his work in the lower house. He was acting almost like a chief whip, ensuring that the government's plans were enacted. When Pitt died Castlereagh resigned but was reappointed to the position by the new Prime Minister, the Duke of Portland.

Nearly every contemporary account of Castlereagh includes a description of his aloofness, his coldness, his lack of human passion. However there is one instance that rather belies this. In 1809, with the backing of Arthur Wellesley, Castlereagh dispatched 40,000 men (including Robert Ross) to the Walcheren region of the Netherlands in an attempt to open another front against the French. It was a disaster as Walcheren Fever literally decimated the force and over 4,000 men died. The expedition had been publicly criticized and privately ridiculed by George Canning, the then Foreign Secretary, although it later emerged that part of the failure was due to his underhand interference with military appointments. With Canning actively conspiring with a weakened Prime Minister behind Castlereagh's back to replace him with Richard Wellesley (who was completely in the dark about the plan), Castlereagh found himself pushed to the limit and he challenged Canning to a duel, which was fought on 21st September 1809. These were two Cabinet ministers firing pistols at each other! Canning missed but Castlereagh hit him in the thigh. Both men resigned. Six months later Canning published a self-serving justification of his actions that inadvertently revealed his true machinations and public opinion, which up until this point had been on his side, swung towards Castlereagh.

Castlereagh remained out of office for three years after the duel. When he did return to office in 1812 it was as Foreign Secretary. He was to hold this position until his death in 1822. However when the then Prime Minister, Spencer Perceval, was assassinated on 11th May 1812, he also took over the role of Leader of the House of Commons. For almost all of Castlereagh's political life there had been either revolution in France or war against Napoleon. Almost the only decent achievement of the late unlamented Spencer Perceval's administration was the decision to keep faith with Arthur Wellesley and his army on the Iberian Peninsula.

Castlereagh had played a key part in the Treaty of Chaumont (March 1814), which formed the quadruple alliance between Britain, Russia, Prussia and Austria and at both the Treaty of Paris and the Congress of Vienna. Many who had been brought up on the ideals of the Enlightenment saw the Congress in particular as a betrayal of the ideas of civil and political liberty, but Castlereagh saw it for what it was – a compromise. The only party at the table who had even the first idea about the reality of parliamentary democracy was Britain. But they were only one part of the negotiations. Again he was held personally responsible for the reactionary regimes that were put in place in Europe, but what realistically could he have done given that he was up against arch conservatives such as the wily Metternich? What he did achieve was more than his political descendants were able to achieve in 1919 at the Treaty of Versailles. At both Paris and Vienna he used all his diplomatic skills to prevent the victorious allies from exacting repressive reparations from the defeated French and restored the borders to the pre-Napoleon ones. He designed the Congress system whereby the main signatory powers met periodically to collectively manage European affairs. Over the next decade there were about five European Congresses and while the meetings petered out following his death in 1822, it could be argued that the peace he had established held until 1914. He had established the principle that Jaw Jaw was better than War War. Henry Kissinger, himself no mean diplomat, says that he developed a reputation for integrity, consistency, and goodwill, which was perhaps unmatched by any diplomat of that era.

Despite his reputation Castlereagh was always inclined towards the centre ground in politics. His experiences in Ireland had shown him the consequences of extremism and this inclination is shown in his support not only for Catholic Emancipation and the Slave Trade Act of 1807. His step-grandfather, Lord Camden, had been a great influence over his political philosophy and it was he, as Attorney General, who had sided with John Wilkes against the government. Why then did Castlereagh, who deplored the events of the Peterloo Massacre on 16 August 1819, get all the blame for the repressive Six Acts that limited not only the right of protest, but also the right to a Free Press and severely limit Free Speech? The answer lies in the fact that he was the only senior member of the government who was in the House of Commons. Both the Prime Minister, Lord Liverpool, and the Home Secretary, Lord Sidmouth (formerly Prime Minister Addington) were in the House of Lords, surrounded by like-minded peers. As had happened in Dublin 20 years earlier he had to take the 'blame' for the policies of others. As Ferdinand Mount says *'he became the incarnation of reaction across a perilously insecure and paranoid United Kingdom'*.

Castlereagh committed suicide on 12 August 1822 by slashing his own throat with a small knife he had hidden in his room. It is now argued that the syphilis that he had contracted at Cambridge University, left untreated, had resulted in madness. He was certainly suffering from a form of paranoia in the days and weeks leading up to his death. At the time his family and doctors thought that he was suffering from nervous exhaustion brought on by the responsibility of leading the House and also the never-ending diplomacy in Europe. He sought refuge from the pressures of work in his country seat, but the paranoia continued. His family hid all his razors and at an audience with George IV on 9th August he told his startled monarch that *"I am accused of the same crime as the Bishop of Clogher."* i.e. homosexuality. However there is no way of telling if this was actually true or simply a delusion such as when he told his friends that he kept seeing a 'radiant boy' in the flames in the fire.

Castlereagh was everyone's whipping boy. He took the flack for the policies and actions of others. He was not the most inspiring of speakers and frequently mangled his sentences along the lines of former President George W Bush. He was the target for all the frustration that intellectuals and the general public felt with a ruling elite that was out of step with public opinion. It could be argued that he could have stepped down and lived a quiet life on the back benches but I think that he preferred to stay to try to make sure that the 'door of mercy' remained open in a reactionary government. In 1791 while still in France he wrote *'When pronouncing on the merits of the constitution we possess, its theoretical principles should not be overlooked, but its practical effects infinitely more deserve our consideration.'* Both Bew and John Derry argue that *'Castlereagh's Irish experience was fundamental to his political attitudes. It explained his profound appreciation of the contrast between romantic oratory and political reality.'*

Certainly there is a lot for which he has to share his portion of the blame, but equally we must not overlook his very real achievements and his aspirations. It is tempting to play 'what if' when looking at his proposals for Catholic Emancipation as part of the Act of Union. And he was the principle architect of a peace accord that lasted for almost a century. Perhaps if there had been a Castlereagh at Versailles in 1919 Blair Mayne could have lived out his life as a rugby-playing solicitor.

A Short History
of Co. Down

This does not even pretend to be a comprehensive history of the county, which would run to several volumes. Instead it is a brief overview of the main periods of interest in the general area now known as Co. Down.

Co. Down ha been inhabited for around 9,000 years and although we don't know their names, our ancestors left their stamp on the countryside with dolmens, standing stones, ring forts, burial cairns and our very own Stonehenge at Ballynoe near Downpatrick.

However the first written records are supplied by the Romans who, although they did not invade Ireland, certainly considered doing so and gathered information about the island and its inhabitants. They told of a cold, damp land peopled by inhospitable and war-like savages. By the second century CE enough information had been accumulated to enable Ptolemy, the great Greek geographer to compile a map of Ireland, despite the fact that he had never visited the island and was based in the slightly warmer climate of

Alexandria, Eygpt. The names of the people and rivers which he uses are remarkably close to the Gaelic names still used today. He records that South Antrim and North Down are the kingdom of the Darini, a name that is reflected in the Irish name for Dundrum – Dún Droma Dáirine. Dario in the Gaulish language meant tumult, rage and agitation, so the Darini may have denoted a warlike or violent people.

By the fifth century Ulstermen started to expand their own territory and invaded Scotland, the Isle of Man and parts of Wales. The kingdom of Dál Riata spread across North Antrim and what is now Argyll facilitating trade between Down and Scotland but in other areas of the western part of what is now England and Wales they contented themselves with raids, snatching local people to bring back to Ireland as slaves. It was on one of these raids in Wales that they grabbed a young man who was to change their world completely. Patrick.

Patrick's conversion to Christianity and mission to Ireland are well known and such was his success that within a surprisingly short time, given the warlike nature of the locals, had established an Irish version of the church in Ireland, with the emphasis on religious studies based in a network of monasteries. These monasteries were to provide a strong base for Christianity at a time when it was under attack elsewhere in Europe. They became centres for learning and produced many of the earliest histories of Ireland as well as beautifully illustrated religious texts. Many of the monasteries were interlinked with students from one either founding or running others in the area and further afield. The monks from the monasteries based in Co. Down, especially those with an association with Bangor Abbey, were responsible for many of the great missions to the rest of Europe in the sixth and seventh centuries CE.

As the monasteries grew in significance so they accumulated great wealth. This was to prove their undoing as it attracted the attention of the fearsome Norsemen of the 9th century. All our accounts of the Vikings and their actions come from their natural enemies – the monks, and so are unlikely to be well balanced unbiased accounts. As a result they tell of black-hearted murderers who cheerfully committed every crime know to early Christian man.

The Vikings were not just content to smash and grab, they were looking for new territory to establish settlements – the foundations of the pier at Groomsport are reputed to date from this time and they also left us the name of one of our loughs Strangford. However, while further south they succeeded in establishing settlements at Dublin and Waterford, in Co. Down they only succeeded in uniting the various warring tribes to come together to fight them and 926 Muircertach (son of Niall Glúndubh) defeated them in a sea battle on Strangford Lough.

The great monasteries of Nendrum, Movilla and Bangor never really recovered from the repeated attacks by the Viking raiders and it was to be another three centuries before they were restored and augmented by another wave of settlers, themselves descended from the Vikings, the Anglo Normans, ruled by the Angevin king Henry II.

As mentioned earlier the church that Patrick established in Ireland had a peculiarly Irish flavour to it, both in litugy and leadership. As far as the church in Ireland was concerned the Gregorian Reforms c1050-80 that had consolidated the power of the church over the laity and centralized power with the Papacy were something that didn't apply to them including the ban on married clergy, something about which the Irish church was more relaxed. St Bernard in his biography of Malachy of Armagh said of the Irish that 'They were Christians in name, in fact pagans.'

One of the main barriers to establishing papal supremacy in Ireland was that there were nine, often competing kingdoms and numerous sub-kingdoms. The role of the High King of Ireland was not hereditary nor was it administrative in a modern sense, which meant that there was no single person with whom to negotiate.

In December 1154 a new Pope was elected, Adrian IV, and when the Archbishop of Canterbury, Theobald of Bec, and his advisor John of Salisbury suggested that one way of getting the Irish Church to come to heel was to appoint the Angevin/English king Henry II as Lord of Ireland, he was more than happy to agree. It was declared that Ireland was to become a fief of the Holy See under the Lordship of the Kings of England. Shortly afterwards barons, mostly from Wales, arrived in Ireland to establish his claim.

From Co. Down's point of view, the most important of these barons was John de Courcy. Despite the fact that almost all the Irish kings had made submission to Henry, Angevin/English influence was confined to a small area hugging the eastern coast of the island and concentrated around Dublin. De Courcy and his friends were determined to carve out a sphere of influence for themselves, away from Dublin and royal authority. They identified the eastern seaboard of what is now Co. Down as their best bet. The coastline provided a connection with de Courcy's father-in-law, the King of the Isle of Man, and the rolling drumlin scattered countryside promised good grazing and farming land.

The attack, in 1177, was unexpected and devastating. The local ruler Rory MacDonleavy fled initially, although he returned with a large army to try to recover his lost property. A savage battle was fought on the banks of the river Quoile, close to Downpatrick, but de Courcy was triumphant. Although he made several other attempts to regain his kingdom over the years, MacDonleavy was not successful.

De Courcy sacked Downpatrick and Armagh capturing all the clergy were captured, the lesser members of the orders killed and the relics and manuscripts belonging to the churches seized. Really this little acorn hadn't fallen that far from his Viking family tree.

Once his power was established de Courcy set about consolidating it by building tower-houses and castles, the ruins of which we still see today. He also started to endow the local churches and it is thanks to him that the monasteries at Nendrum and Inch were restored. He also built and endowed Downpatrick Cathedral and transferred what were thought to be the bones of saints Patrick, Brigid and Colmcille to the new Cathedral. His wife Affreca established the Cistercian monastery at Greyabbey. All these new ecclesiastical establishments were run by monks from England and France, which meant that the local church stayed within the control of the centralized church system.

De Courcy and his supporters established their hold on the area around the Ards peninsula and Lecale and if that had been the extent of their activities it is likely that they would have been left alone. However, de Courcy began to get delusions of grandeur and thought that he could emulate the local Irish kings. His most serious mistake was when he started to mint his own coins, with his own image on them rather than the King. This was a step too far and King John (brother of Richard the Lionheart), who was not the most forgiving of rulers at the best of times, was forced to act against him. He enlisted the help of Hugh de Lacy (from Meath) to wage war on de Courcy. A vicious war ensued, fought exclusively by the settlers, after which de Courcy was driven out of Ulster and on 29 May 2015 Hugh was created Earl of Ulster.

There are various stories about de Courcy's strength that have come down through the centuries. Perhaps the best known is the story in the Book of Howth about his capture by de Lacy. De Courcy had taken sanctuary in the church at Downpatrick so de Lacy approached some of his men to ask them to turn their coats and take him prisoner. Given that de Courcy 'lived ever in his armour' they devised a plan to try to take him on Good Friday when he would be bare-footed and without either armour or weapons. *And so they came at him upon the sudden, and he had no shift to make but with the cross pole, and defended him until it was broken and slew thirteen of them before he was taken.'*

De Courcy made various attempts to regain his lost 'kingdom' before his death c1219, and even accompanied King John to Ireland in 1210 to oust de Lacy who had fallen out of favour with the king, but he never regained his previous territory and influence. Affreca is thought to have lived out her widowhood in Greyabbey and is buried there.

English rule continued with families such as the Savages and de Burghs holding the land together with powerful Irish families who had pragmatically accepted that they owned a nominal allegiance to the occupant of the English throne. To the average Irish peasant it really made little difference if their land was owned by an Irish, English or Church landlord, their lives were pretty miserable anyway and besides they had more important matters to worry about as there were recurring famines and plagues including the Black Death to occupy their minds.

As if the Black Death wasn't enough to worry about in 1315, encouraged by his military successes against the English in the north of England, Robert the Bruce invaded Ireland, supposedly to free the country from English rule at the request of Irish kings. In 1316 his brother Edward was crowned as High King of Ireland. Bruce had a vision of a 'Pan-Gaelic Greater Scotia' with a united kingdom of Scotland and Ireland – ruled by his own family of course. His wife was a de Burgh, the family who were then the Earls of Ulster, and he claimed descent from the great Brian Boru himself. In a letter to the Irish kings he stressed their common heritage, common language etc and referred to *nostra nacio* – our nation.

This argument appealed to the Ulster kings, for whom it made sense, although the rest of Ireland wasn't so sure. In fact when Edward was defeated and killed at the battle of Faughart (14

October 1318) the Irish Annals of the period described the defeat of the Bruces by the English as one of the greatest things ever done for the Irish nation due to the fact it brought an end to the famine and pillaging wrought upon the Irish by both the Scots and the English.

When contemplating the history of the area known as County Down there is a immediate hurdle to pass. Although Ireland was divided into counties in the twelfth century, for most of its history Co. Down was in fact divided into separate parts. Up until the early seventeenth century the north-east was ruled by various different families who were part of the larger territory of Dál Fiatach and Uliad, whereas the south-west, Iveagh, was under the control of the Magennis family and the south-east was under the control of the descendants of medieval settlers. And that is before one starts to unravel the various other interested parties from Robert the Bruce to (bad) King John of England.

Bruce had been supported by the Magennis (Mac Aionghusa) family who ruled over the territory known as Iveagh from around about 1140. Prior to that date the territory had been controlled by the Ua hAitidhe or Haughey family who, to their detriment, had developed the nasty habit of killing whoever from the family had drawn the short straw and been elected king. The Magennis's were a branch of this family who had managed to not only gain control from the wider Haughey family, but also to restrain from killing their elected kings. This undoubtedly made family weddings and gatherings more convivial, but also allowed them to consolidate their power and withstand encroachments in the late 12th century and beyond by de Courcy, de Lacy et al. Based in Rathfriland they used the confusion offered by Bruce's invasion to expand their territory as far east as Dundrum, which gave them access to the sea.

By 1485 when Henry Tudor defeated Richard III at Bosworth, one of the most powerful families in Co. Down was the O'Neill family of Clandeboye. They were part of a larger clan who had a great influence on the history of Ulster. In 1449 Henry O'Neill had backed the wrong horse in the War of the Roses when he recognised Henry VI as his liege lord in return for being acknowledged as overlord of Ulster with permission to attack all those who refused to submit to his rule.

Henry VII did make attempts to re-establish his control over Ireland but he was more concerned with consolidating his power in England. His son Henry VIII was a different matter. He was not the first of the English kings to lay claim to Ireland but he was the first to determine to really rule it. One of the most obvious effects that this had in Co. Down was the dissolution of the monasteries in 1539. The break with Rome did not cause as much of an outcry as would at first be supposed. Despite the close links with the wider European, Rome centred church, which had been established under de Courcy, the church in Ireland had fallen back into its old ways. Celibacy was rare, the clergy took sides in the various disputes and some cases were actively involved. The O'Neills were not convinced that it was worth making much of a fuss and anyway, initially, it did not make that much of a difference. It was not until Elizabeth came to the throne in 1558 that the effects of the Reformation and Counter-Reformation started to take on any significance.

One of the methods used by Henry to get control was the system of 'surrender and regrant' policy operated by the Tudor state. This was a policy whereby the Irish kings/chieftains were offered the opportunity to guarantee their property under English common law, rather than the Brehon law system, then operating in Ireland. The plan was to persuade Irish ruling families to surrender their lands to the English crown and they would then have them regranted as freeholds under a royal charter if they swore loyalty to the English monarch. In return they would be protected from attack and could enter the Parliament of Ireland. By agreeing to go down this route it meant that the Irish families, and more importantly their land, were protected by the political and constitutional system in the rest of England, where everyone was equal at law under the monarch. It was only through acts of open rebellion against the crown that their land could be seized.

Meanwhile the Magennis family had fallen back into their old ways of squabbling amongst themselves and cattle raiding. When in 1539 a cattle raid in Meath led to them being defeated by the Lord Deputy of Ireland's forces, Art Magennis decided that he should take advantage of 'surrender and regrant' and in 1543 did just this. He travelled over to Greenwich Palace to be knighted by Henry VIII and returned as Sir Arthur Guiness. His successor Hugh Magennis (not his heir in a primogeniture sense) success-fully petitioned Elizabeth I in 1575 and received his knighthood and confirmation of his right of tenure over 'the entire country or territory of Iveagh.' Despite the Iveagh Magennis's remaining neutral in the Nine Years War (1594-1603) their land was split into 15 freeholds. They family retained 13 of them, but the other two were given to officers of the crown who had served under Sir Arthur Chichester and Sir Henry Bagenal, who had acquired land around Newry. The Guinness family still retain the title of Earl of Iveagh today.

Whereas in post reformation England the Government was able to enforce a ban on priests, in Ireland they were unable to prevent them from returning to the country. These new priests were a dif-ferent breed to the ones who had been expelled originally. They had been trained in Europe and were filled with all the fervour of missionaries and fired by the efforts being made at a Counter-Reformation. Of more significance was that when Elizabeth and her ministers turned their attention to Ireland and decided that they should make more concerted efforts at settlement the people who were sent to settle the land were protestant.

Initially the dominant family in Down, the O'Neills, tried to make some sort of arrangement with Elizabeth. Shane O'Neill was summoned to London in 1562 to see Elizabeth and explain his attacks on the Earl of Sussex. He struck an uneasy peace with her but soon after his return to Ireland he was once more up to his old tricks and attacking local families. He attacked the MacDonnells of the Glens of Antrim, ostensibly to regain the Queen's favour. Whatever his professed intentions the end result was that he was the de facto ruler of Ulster outside English control. The English authorities were saved the effort of trying to capture O'Neill when he was hacked to death during a feast with the MacDonnells but following his death Elizabeth and her ministers decided to embark on the Plantation of Ireland to prevent the possibility of the rise of a similar figure.

One of these settlers was a Privy councillor and vice-chancellor at Cambridge, Sir Thomas Smith. Somehow Smith and his son obtained letters patent to the lands of Clandeboye. This was despite the fact that Sir Brian MacPhelim O'Neill had fought against Shane and been knighted for his service to the crown. Smith made clear his intention to clear the land of all the native Irish, except for those who could be used to till the soil. Presumably this policy was to include Sir Brian who did not wait to find out. When Sir Thomas's son, also Thomas, landed at Strangford in August 1572 with approximately 100 fellow colonists, Sir Brian put a scorched earth policy into effect. He burnt and destroyed every building which might be used for shelter by the English – even the churches and abbeys were destroyed. Smith's appeals for help to the new Lord Deputy, Sir William Fitzwilliam went unheeded as Fitzwilliam had been vehemently opposed to the expedition from the start. The hapless Smith was murdered in Comber by his own Irish servants in 1573.

Sir Brian had an equally grisly end. He had made his peace with the Earl of Essex, who had been granted most of Co Antrim, and invited him to a feast in Belfast Castle. After three days of feasting the guests turned on their hosts and Sir Brian, his wife and brother were all arrested and sent to Dublin where they were hung, drawn and quartered as traitors to the crown.

By the time Elizabeth died in 1603 and was succeeded by James VI of Scotland the O'Neill's of Clandeboye remained as the main landowners in most of the north of the county. Rev J O'Laverty the author of *Diocese of Down and Connor: Ancient and modern* points out that while one might suspect that the natives were delighted to be ruled by their own after the centuries of interference by English and Scots alike, the reality was not quite what they might wish for. *'Unfortunately they adhered to the Celtic system of electing their chief from among the members of the dominant family (tanistry) ... This elective principle in the choice of their chiefs led to bloodshed and ruinous contests on the death of each chief'.*

Keith Haines in his excellent book *Knock, Knock ... who was there?* admits that

> *'The Gaelic control of Upper Clandeboye and the Great Ards (effectively north Down) during the last quarter of the 16th century is confusing. There must have been some suspicion amongst the O'Neill clan that this was something of a poisoned chalice.'*

In fact it is possible to have something approaching a minor breakdown trying to remember which O'Neill is which and whose son, nephew or grandson they were. The only easy aspect of this time is that they were all men. No woman need apply.

For our purposes all we need to know is that at the time of Elizabeth's death in 1603 the O'Neill in control of the northern part of Co. Down was Conn O'Neill who as Keith Haines prosaically puts it 'was conned'.

There is a valid reason for concentrating on the [mis]adventures of Conn, as the consequences led to the subsequent 'Plantation' of Co. Down having a tartan tinge, as the majority of the settlers were Scottish, and Presbyterian. Certainly in the south of the county there were English families such as the Annesleys in Castlewellan who were later joined in the late 17th and early 18th century by Hugeonots, but by and large the settlers were Scottish Presbyterians and this was to be very important in shaping the physical and economic landscape over the following centuries.

At the time of Elizabeth's death Conn was a prisoner in Carrickfergus Castle. He, his brothers and friends had been on a bit of a binge at Castlereagh when they started to run out of supplies. He sent a number of slightly more sober servants to Belfast to get some more wine, but they had got into a fight with some English soldiers and returned empty handed. Conn sent them back, but this time armed and in the resulting brawl a solider was killed. As Haines points out this was a 'trivial skirmish' and should not have been taken further, but tension between the settlers and the natives meant that Chichester (later Lord Deputy of Ireland and founder of modern day Belfast), who was not favourably disposed towards the Irish Chieftains following the decapitation of his older brother John by the MacDonnells in 1597 (they reputedly used his head as a football), chose to believe that this was not a drunken brawl but rather the opening salvos in a treasonable plot by Conn against the crown. O'Neill was found guilty and imprisoned in Carrickfergus Castle.

A couple of years before this event Hugh Montgomery of Braidstane (Broadstone) in Ayrshire and his wider family had started up a commercial business centred around Carrickfergus. Not only was Montgomery involved in trade but he, and another key player in our story, and James Hamilton were also almost certainly secret agents for James VI of Scotland, who was soon to inherit the English crown. There are various stories surrounding the ensuing events but what it certain is that Montgomery promised to assist Conn to escape and gain a pardon from James VI (I) in return for half his estate. The most romantic story has Conn's second wife Eilis Ni Neill smuggling ropes into the castle in two large hollowed out cheeses. Once Conn was safely in Scotland the more wily Hamilton managed to petition the new King of England for his share of O'Neill's land as well.

It remains a mystery as to why Conn agreed to this deal. There is an argument that O'Neill did not own the land in a manner, which was recognised by the English administration. His claim to the land was through tanistry rather than primogeniture, so by giving Montgomery and Hamilton most of North Down and Ards, he was gaining legal rights over what was left. Also, he knew that the area that he was giving away had never recovered from the scorced earth policy of Sir Brian O'Neill thirty years previously. In fact the Montgomery Manuscript reports that when the Scottish settlers arrived they found that *'30 cabins could not be found, nor any stone walls, but ruined roofless churches a... and a stump of an old castle in Newtown, in each of which some Gentlemen sheltered themselves at their first coming over.'* Even Sir Hugh Montgomery and his family had to rough it initially when they arrived to claim their new estates in the summer of 1608, *'some of the priory walls were roofed and fitter for his lady and children and servants to live in.'* By the time that he died in 1619, Conn had mismanaged his remaining land to such an extent that it was greatly reduced. His son, Daniel, did attempt to regain control over the land that his father had given away or sold but to no avail. The county was now subdivided into estates and farms that changed the physical appearance of the land forever.

Given the outbreaks of violence which greeted attempts at plantation elsewhere in Ireland, and indeed in the southern part of Co.
Down, the settlement around Lecale and Ards was remarkably free
from tension. One reason may have been that due to the almost
constant conflict and the resulting famines of the latter years of the
sixteenth century, large swathes of the county had been depopulated and so there was no-one to displace. Also the people who
arrived to settle the land were not English, but rather Scots who
some of whom spoke a similar language. Rev J. O'Laverty tells of
them hiding priests and when the penal laws were at their height,
of registering their tenants under suitably protestant sounding
names. Of course, as Presbyterians they themselves fell foul of the
penal laws, but more of that later.

This is not to say that there were no tensions. Certainly the introduction of settlers who were of a different religious denomina-
tion was bound to heighten fears on both sides at times of strife
elsewhere in the country. During the 1641 rebellion the southern
part of the county saw some of the fiercest fighting and greatest
atrocities, on both sides of the conflict and it was at this time that
Bloody Bridge in the Mournes acquired its name. Many of the
people who rallied to try to expel the new settlers were themselves
the descendants of the old Anglo-Norman settlers from 300 years
before and many forfeited their estates.

The situation was further confused at this time by the English Civil
War, which pitted Royalists, who supported Charles I (Scottish)
against the Parliamentarians led by Oliver Cromwell. It was to crush
all Royalist dissent that Cromwell arrived in Ireland in 1649. Most
of the Scottish settlers were royalists and they raised an army to
oppose the Parliamentary forces. At a battle near Lisburn they were
completely defeated and Montgomery and Hamilton, amongst
others, forfeited their estates, although they were restored to them

in 1660 after the restoration of the Stuart crown. This then was the world into which Sir Hans Sloane was born in Killyleagh.

The seventeenth century was one of rebellion and unrest in Ireland in general. As the colonisation of the island continued apace, so the sectarian divides became more rigid and acquired the weight of law. Most significantly the majority of the settlers in Co. Down, who were Presbyterian, found that they were being punished for the sins of Cromwell's Parliamentarians and that the laws which began to be introduced placing restrictions on religious freedom applied as much to them as to their Catholic neighbours. This led to a development of mistrust of authority, which was to have great significance a century later.

The Williamite Wars certainly raised religious tensions in the area. The population was again gripped with fears of massacre and thus many were willing recruits to both armies when Schomberg's army landed in Bangor. King William himself is reputed to have made camp in Scarva on his way south towards the Boyne river, an event that is still celebrated in modern times with the annual Sham Fight in the grounds of Scarvagh House on the 13th of July. In the event for the majority of the population, ie the Roman Catholics and Presbyterians, the success of the protestant William was to make little change in their lives. If anything in respect of the so-called Penal Laws, things got worse as they were debarred from political involvement as well as all the other petty restrictions on inheritance, recognition of marriages, bearing of arms and ownership of horses etc.

Despite this, in a country that lived under almost constant fear of 'papish revolt', for the most part the various petty restrictions on Non-conformists were not strictly adhered to. It would not do to completely alienate such a large portion of your potential allies and in the second half of the eighteenth century the Patriot Party, under the leadership of Henry Grattan, were committed to the repeal of the Penal Laws and universal [male] emancipation. The first half of the eighteenth century also saw a period of great want. There were a series of crop failures and plagues and the spectre of famine stalked the land.

It is thought that the number of people who died during this famine is comparable to the number who died in the Great Famine of the next century and as they were to do almost a century later many sought to leave the country altogether. There was a dramatic increase in the number of immigrants to the American colonies at this time. They went for a variety of reasons, but chief amongst them was the promise of a better life and these settlers were to have a profound influence on events in their new land.

Towards the end of the century there were two major developments elsewhere in the world which were to have a dramatic effect on life in Ulster. The first was the American colonies' War of Independence which began with the Declaration of Independence on 4th July 1776. Although the government in Dublin was horrified by this revolt against the crown, the population of Co. Down was very interested in the news for entirely different reasons. Many of the rebels were their own kinsmen and women and the Belfast Newsletter carried daily reports from the colonies. The effects were not just felt at one remove. In April 1778 the residents of North Down were alarmed to see the American ship 'Ranger' sail into Belfast Lough and attack and seize HMS Drake.

The residents of the county were torn. There was a call by the Patriot Party for volunteers as the country was rapidly emptied of regular troops who were dispatched to fight in the colonies. The Volunteers were to prove a useful tool for the party who wanted greater autonomy for the Dublin Parliament and Grattan referred to them as 'the armed property of the nation'. He and his party were committed to gradual reform, however, something which was treated with suspicion by radicals in Co. Down and elsewhere in the north. These radicals were inspired by the ideals set forward by the other great event in the closing decades of the eighteenth century – the French Revolution.

Again the Belfast Newsletter carried daily reports from France and the ideals of brotherhood, liberty and freedom struck a chord with their readership. The Belfast Volunteers sent a message of support to Paris and the new ideas were widely discussed. The eighteenth century was the age of Enlightenment and one of the leading centres for the new ideas were the Scottish universities. Thanks to the Penal Laws, Presbyterians in Ireland were not allowed to attend Trinity College, Dublin and so anyone wishing to train in Medicine, Law or Theology had to go to Scotland for their degrees. It should have come as no surprise, therefore, when they were all caught up in the new radical political ideas.

The United Irishmen were formed in 1791 in Belfast. Initially they were tolerated by the authorities. They ran their own newspaper, the Northern Star, which concentrated on local news and was soon attracting articles by some of the leading radicals, amongst them Rev James Porter of Greyabbey, Rev William Steele Dickson from Ballyhalbert and Rev Thomas Ledlie Birch of Saintfield. The involvement of the Presbyterian clergy was crucial in the support which the movement was able to attract in Co Down and Co Antrim. Elsewhere in Ulster the local population was roughly 50-50 but in both Antrim and Down there was a very marked protestant majority. In fact in certain areas the population was almost 100% protestant. They could therefore afford to be more tolerant of new ideas and in fact in the eastern part of the county the local Presbyterian communities were very active champions of local Catholics. Elsewhere the situation was not so relaxed. Secret societies such as the Peep-o-day boys [protestant] and the Defenders [catholic] were constantly engaging in skirmishes. This came to a head in 1795 at the battle of the Diamond in Loughgall, just across the country border, which led to the founding of the Orange Order.

The rising in the summer of 1798 was to split the countryside, pitting family members against each other and landlords against tenants. Two of the most important battles were fought at Saintfield and Ballynahinch and nearly every family in the county had someone on either side. The United Irishmen were particularly well supported in the Ards peninsula, which was also home to their chief opponent, Lord Castlereagh who was ruthless in crushing the revolt. In time he was successful and the rising's only lasting effect was to hasten the political union between Ireland and the rest of Great Britain, which happened in 1801.

County Down did not lend itself readily to industry but what it did have was a naturally fertile soil and temperate climate, which made the growing of crops and grazing of animals relatively easy. It also had miles of coastline, which made trade with other parts of the kingdom relatively easy. However, traditional farming was still a precarious and not very profitable occupation. There was one crop however which could change all that. Flax.

The fertile countryside and good irrigation made the growing and processing of flax relatively easy. Initially the linen industry was run on a very small scale but an influx of Huguenot and Flemish refugees bringing great textile skills into the province in the early eighteenth century accelerated its development. Farmers were able to augment their income by weaving their own cloth and selling it at market. Soon nearly every market town in the county had a linen hall and the trade was encouraged and assisted by developments in communications. The Newry Canal was opened in 1742, the ports of Donaghadee and Belfast were thriving and, more importantly after 1801 there was a period of relative peace, which helped the development of economic prosperity. By 1886 G H

Bassett was able to state that *'Down is now by far the largest flax-growing county in Ulster.'*

Linen gave farmers a cushion to protect them from the fluctuations in agriculture that were outside their control. Everyone in the family could contribute to the family coffers, including the women. As late as the mid-twentieth century wives and daughters could earn extra income by hand embroidering fine linen at home. Mr and Mrs S C Hall, writing in 1846, said that

> *'Through the whole of this district – the barony of Ards and that of Castlereagh – a large proportion of the peasantry are employed in what is technically termed 'flowering' – embroidering muslin chiefly for the Glasgow manufacturer … The workers earn generally about 3 shillings a week, a small sum, but as the majority of the inmates of a cottage are similarly employed sufficient is obtained to procure the necessities of life; and indeed some of its luxuries for the interiors of many of the cabins present all aspects of cheerfulness and comfort.'*

Mr and Mrs Hall's visit to Co. Down coincided with one of the greatest disasters to face not only the county but also Ireland as a whole. I am constantly surprised by the number of people who appear to think that either the north of the country avoided the great Potato Famine or that somehow the blight was confined to catholic potatoes alone. In fact the potato blight had first appeared in Co. Antrim and soon crossed the Belfast Lough. The Ards peninsula was particularly badly hit and up to a third of the population of Carrowdore was wiped out by the diseases that spread through the weakened population. The newly opened workhouses in all the counties major market towns such as Downpatrick, Newry, Lisburn and Newtownards were swamped by people seeking assistance from the state. The situation was made worse by the fact that it coincided with an economic downturn as handloom weavers were finding it increasingly difficult to compete with the technological developments in the industry.

However the worse effects of the disaster were mitigated by the fact that the large towns did possess industries which could provide alternative employment, not only in the Linen industry but also ship-building, rope making etc, and by the fact that the system of land tenure in Ulster was different to that elsewhere on the island and gave tenant farmers more security. This meant that prior to the potato blight appearing there was not the same level of subsistence farming as elsewhere and so there was a greater range of crops. As always, emigration could offer an escape from hardship at home.

Despite the very real suffering experienced during the Famine, the county in general began to prosper throughout the nineteenth century. Advances in technology, especially the railway, not only helped trade in the area but also provided an alternative source of employment. The growth of the large towns such as Lisburn, Newtownards and Newry and their factories and shops, provided an alternative to emigration. The increased prosperity led to an attendant growth in the 'middle class', which in turn led to im-provements in education and provision of health. While for those at the bottom of society life was still rather ghastly, with the threat of the workhouse an ever present spectre, farmers sons and daugh-ters were now able to seek employment and advancement within easy travelling distance from their homesteads, rather than across a large body of water.

The railways also brought welcome income to previously remote areas of the county such as the Mournes. Newcastle developed into a holiday resort for the professional classes and the writings and paintings of Percy French brought fresh interest in the area. Towns such as Bangor were reborn as holiday destinations and dormitory towns for the nearby Belfast. Increased prosperity also brought in-creased leisure and interest in the past. It was in the second half of the nineteenthth century that many of the sporting clubs in the county were founded including GAA clubs.

The start of the twentieth century saw exciting new technology and engineering, such as aeroplanes and motorcars. Two of the most famous of our local sons, James Martin and Harry Ferguson, both came from farms in the county. The increased prosperity also led to the burgeoning of the professional classes and for the first time these were open to both sexes. Harry Ferguson's two aunts became doctors and leading lights in the women's suffrage movement. Employment outside the home and farm led to women demanding to take a full part in the political life of the country. Nowhere was this more obvious than in the demand for and opposition to the Home Rule bill of the early decades of the century.

While many will be familiar with the formation of the Ulster Volunteer Force and Carson's Ulster Covenant, which drew support from men and women across the province committed to maintaining the political union with the United Kingdom, what is not so well known is the support of some sections of the protestant community for Home Rule.

One of the leading proponents for this was Alice Milligan. A fluent Irish speaker, Alice was originally from Omagh but she and her family spent most of her life living on Clifton Road in Bangor. One wonders what the members of the Methodist church in Bangor thought when they learnt of her house guests and friends, who comprised a who's who of the Nationalist and later Republican movement in Ireland including Maud Gonne, James Connolly, Francis Joseph Biggar and Roger Casement. Alice was actually with Casement when he received news about his knighthood. She also travelled with him to Larne in April 1914 after the gunrunning incident, which Harry Ferguson took part in, although she could have stayed closer to home as guns were brought in to Bangor the same year. Bangor born Winifred Carney and Alice were founding members of Sinn Fein and friends of James Connolly. Winifred was actually in the GPO in 1916 acting as an assistant to Connolly. She refused to leave his side when others sought to escape.

Not only were sons and daughters of the county involved in the increasingly violent political struggle at home, but both sides of the community flocked to volunteer to fight in the First World War. The 36th Ulster Division trained within sight of Helen's Tower and Scrabo and saw action throughout the war to end all wars. As news filtered through in July 1916 there was scarcely a townland in the county who had not had a father, son or grandson involved in the Battle of the Somme and every town and village has its own memorial to those who were killed in the 1914-18 war.

The inter war years saw great political and economic upheavals in the county. The partition of Ireland meant that Newry became a border town. In the 1921 election for the new Northern Ireland House of Commons the county was given 8 seats, which were contested by the single transferable vote method of proportional representation. James Craig topped the poll in the first count with 29,829 and Eamon de Valera came second with 21,677. After the final count 6 Unionist candidates were returned along with de Valera (Sinn Fein) and Patrick O'Neill (Nationalist). After 1929 the county was further divided into 8 constituencies, which ran along traditional county boundaries, Ards, East Down, Iveagh, Mid Down, Mourne, North Down, South Down and West Down. In the 6 subsequent elections up to 1949 six of the constituencies returned Ulster Unionist MPs. The exceptions were Mourne, which returned Nationalist MPs and South Down. De Valera contested the 1933 election in South Down as a Fianna Fáil candidate and won 92.3% of the vote. He did not take his seat. In the 1938 election James Brown, who ran as an Independent Unionist, won with 93.6% of the vote. Other than these two elections the constituency always returned a Nationalist MP.

The worldwide depression in the 1930s hit the linen and related industries in the county. Agriculture was not exempt and there was real hardship for many. As ever the main export of the county was its young people, who boarded boats to all four corners of the world a traffic which continues to the present day. The Second World War brought the realities of the German Blitz to the county as Bangor was bombed during the Easter raids in 1941and a German plane was shot down just outside the bay after it had dropped its payload on the seaside town and machine-gunned men walking up Main Street towards the train station. As was the case in the First World War, men and women in the county volunteered to serve in the Armed Forces and the most decorated soldier of the war, Blair Mayne, came from Newtownards.

Throughout the ages, since the first settlers arrived on its shores, the people of County Down have shaped the physical and political landscape of their country. In the course of researching the individuals discussed in this book certain themes have emerged that link most, if not all of them. The greatest of these is an unshakable belief that what they were doing was correct. If they were out of step with the rest of the world, then it was up to the world to catch up, they were not going to compromise. This was as true of Amy Carmichael in India as it was of the ancient saints Patrick, Comgall and Columbanus. It shines through the lives of Henry Martin and Harry Ferguson as much as that of Margaret Byers and Elizabeth Bell. Another trait is great personal bravery. Blair Mayne, Frank Pantridge, Robert Ross and Rollo Gillespie were the true heirs of the heroes of the Ulster Cycle and Cú Chulainn. This county has never been just one people. It has been enriched by successive waves of settlers, some have come in peace, some have not, but all have shaped who we are today.

Bibliography

If you are interested in getting a more detail account of the various personalities included in this book, may I suggest that you track down copies of the following books and articles. There are also a few websites that can give more information.

Barker, J. (2010) *The Brontës*, 2nd edn,. London: Abacus.

Best, C. (2015) *Second Best: My Dad and Me* London: Transworld

Best, G. (2012) *Blessed: Autobiography* London: Ebury

Bew, J. (2011) *Castlereagh: The Biography of a Statesman* Kindle Edition, Riverrun

Brooke, E. S. (1954) *Sir Hans Sloane: The Great Collector and His Circle* London: Batchworth Press.

Bullock, S. F. (1999) *Thomas Andrews Shipbuilder* Belfast: Blackstaff Press Ltd;

Clarke, M. (2009) *Harry Ferguson before the plough* Donaghadee: Ballyhay Books

Cunningham, S. B. (2016) *Sir Crawford McCullagh: Belfast's Dick Whittington* Donaghadee: Ballyhay Books

Delbourgo, J. (2017) *Collecting the world: The Life and Curiosity of Hans Sloane* London: Allen Lane (Penguin).

Ellis, S. (2018), *Take Courage: Anne Brontë and the Art of Life,* London: Vintage.

Fraser, C. (1973) *Harry Ferguson, Inventor and Pioneer* Ipswich: Old Pond Publishing Ltd.

Gaskell, E (1971) *Life of Charlotte Brontë,* London: reprinted by The Folio Society

Green, D. (2010) *Patrick Brontë: Father of Genius,* Stroud: History Press

Haines, K. (1993) *Neither Rogues Nor Fools: A history of Campbell College and Campbellians* Belfast: Nicholson & Bass Ltd.

Haines, K. (2014) *Knock, Knock, who was there– A brief history of Knock, Belmont & Strandtown and the people who lived there* Donaghadee: Ballyhay Books

Hamilton, D. Jordan, A. (1990) *Margaret Byers: pioneer of women's education and founder of Victoria College Belfast,* Belfast: Institute of Irish Studies.

MacIntyre, B. (2016) *SAS: Rogue Heroes – the Authorized Wartime History* London: Penguin

McGrath, A. (2013) *C S Lewis: A Life: Eccentric Genius, Reluctant Prophet* London: Hodder and Stoughton

Murray I. H. (2015) *Amy Carmichael: Beauty for Ashes, a biography* Edinburgh: Banner of Truth Trust

Pantridge, F. (1989) *An Unquiet Life: Memoirs of a physician and cardiologist.* Antrim: Greystone Books.

BIBLIOGRAPHY

Riddell, F (2018) *Death in ten minutes: Kitty Marion, Activist, Arsonist, Suffragette* London: Hodder and StoughtonRoss, H. (2011) *Paddy Mayne: Lt Col Blair 'Paddy' Mayne, 1 SAS Regiment* Stroud: History Press

Sharman. S. (1996) *Sir James Martin: The authorized biography of the Martin-Baker ejection seat pioneer* Yeovil: Patrick Stephens Limited

Snow, P. (2013) *When Britain Burned the White House: The 1814 Invasion of Washington* London: John Murray

Thorn, Major Sir W. (1816) *A Memoir of Sir R. R. Gillespie.* Major Sir William Thorn, London. Available as a .pdf at www.irishmasonichistory.com

Articles and .pdfs

Her Story I, II, III: profiles of Ulster-ScotsWomen; Ulster-Scots Community Network.

Stanley A Hawkins *The Life of Sir Hans Sloane* in the Ulster Medical Journal [2010 Jan: 79(1) 25-29]

Lynn René Bayley *Irish Girl Got the Blues* published online at www.artmusiclounge. wordpress.com/2016/03/21/irish-girl-got-the-blues

Julian, D. *Frank's Legacy from an European Perspective* in the Ulster Medical Society Journal v79 (Suppl.1); 2010 January.

Review of the J. Frank Patridge Festschrift. Irish Medical Journal. June 1987

Lady Doctors of the Malta Garrison – Elizabeth Bell

Shelagh-Mary Rea: *Dr Elizabeth Gould Bell (1862-1934) – The First Woman To Graduate In Medicine And Practice In Ulster:* Ulster Medical Journal 2017 Sep; 86(3); 189-195

L. Leneman: *Medical Women in the first world war – ranking nowhere:* BMJ v307(6919); 1993 Dec. 18

Gordon Lucy: *Elizabeth Gould Bell: Feminist trailblazer whose life was sadly blighted by family tragedy.* Belfast NewsLetter 13 August 2018

Websites

www.ulster-scots.com
www.newulsterbiography.co.uk
www.chrisbarber.net
www.comberhistory.com
www.martinwardsbooks.com
www.ncbi.nlm.nih.gov
www.maltaramc.com

Other sources

Natural History Heroes, BBC Radio 4.
In Our Time, BBC Radio 4.

Dear Reader,

I hope you have enjoyed this publication from Ballyhay Books, an imprint of Laurel Cottage Ltd. We publish an eclectic mix of books ranging from personal memoirs to authoritative books on local history, from sport to poultry, from photographs to fiction and from music to marine interests – but all with a distinctly local flavour.

To see details of these books, as well as the beautifully illustrated books of our sister imprint Cottage Publications, why not visit our website **www.cottage-publications.com** or telephone +44 (0)28 9188 8033.

Timothy J Johnston

BALLYHAY BOOKS